T!ME...

How life's story
became your story

LOUISE L. KALLAWAY

T!ME…
How life's story became your story

First published in Australia by Louise L. Kallaway 2024
louiselkallaway.com

A catalogue record for this
book is available from the
National Library of Australia

ISBN: 978-0-6459194-5-5 (pbk)

Typesetting and design by Publicious Book Publishing
Published in collaboration with Publicious Book Publishing
www.publicious.com.au

Louise L . Kallaway

I dedicate *T!ME...* to The Universe, time, self-respect, Higher consciousness and wisdom.

'The system' we inherited empowered 'The group'.

Conforming with the rules of 'The Group'

is the #1 issue in all stages of our lives…

until we have the courage to liberate our
freedom from 'The system'.

Louise L. Kallaway.

THE POWER RIDE

INTRODUCTION

Hello and welcome to *T!me…* a survival perspective.

How life's story became your story is a real-life adventure into time and how two completely different periods i.e., Caveman and the 21st Century, non-intellectual and intellectual respectively, are connected and how we live in the same system, on 'autopilot' today.

The 21st Century is not separate… it is part of time and life's story.

We are taking on Goliath… 'A Survival System' originating thousands of years ago. Today, it is dumbing us down and stunting 'The individual' as we live a *much longer lifespan* with an evolving intellectual brain.

***

What inspires you? I write almost every day. Watching a book or journal come to life from its conception to the collation and flow of its contents and building a powerful positive conclusion is a truly enjoyable and motivational experience for me.

What's your story? We all have a unique story. When did *your* story start? The moment you were born? a generation earlier? the moment life began?

Have you given any thought to the origins of life? e.g.,

- Did life begin without a structure? Without rules? Without Laws?

- Was any thought given to the survival of all species?

- Was there no preparation? Nothing organised? No programs operating?

- Are we just a random happening?

- How did we survive without an intellectual brain?

- Did fear evolve over time or was it borne into our DNA?

I believe life is very structured; that survival programs are a gift, bestowed upon the living by The Universe.

What will you allow into your imagination? Do you have rules? Must everything be scientifically proven before your intellectual brain and/or your ego will accept a new concept or a theory? Do you allow 'unproven' to enter your life? Never, sometimes… depends?

Resistance is one thing; flat-out denial completely locks and blocks further information on that subject from entering your consciousness.

How do you come to your conclusions?

- Do you simply *react* and block the concept? Or

- Do you take your time, sift through available information, then *respond?*

Therein lies a powerful realisation and essentially, the essence of this book.

***

I love wisdom! I have written six Non-fiction books and journals to date bringing survival intelligence and its forces into the 21st Century to make sense of our lives. On a trusted friend's suggestion, hello Trish, I am writing Life's Story in both Non-fiction and Fiction categories this time. Fact or fiction… you be the judge.

With my 30-years of research into 'The systems' we were born into, I believe ONCE UPON A T!ME… and its love-child, T!ME… are closer to the truth about our programmed lives, than ever before.

***

The main objective of these two books is to bring you to a considered level of self-respect and Higher Consciousness:

- **Respect for yourself as a Child; all you had to learn day after day, all the *conforming* rules and all the standards expected of you.**

- **Respect for yourself as a Teenager; trying to fit in and to be accepted by your 'tight' peer group/generation and its pressures to *conform*, while trying to separate from your childhood family and its *conformity* expectations.**

- **Respect for yourself, a maturing adult, so hammered into submission by *conformity*, fear, rules and conditioning all learnt in the first half of your life, that you now feel 'stuck' and powerless in midlife and labelled as 'having a Crisis' should you choose to defy 'the rules' and live your life on your terms!**

***

Should I touch on anything that causes you concern, please talk with a trusted friend or counsellor. Watch for any signs of resistance; your confidant may be in denial. You have the power and the free will as a maturing adult to make your own decisions today… with or without anyone's approval. *Remember that!*

I have chosen to use the masculine 'he' or 'him' rather than 'he/she', 'him/her'. There is no gender bias, it simply makes for an easier read.

Enjoy *T!me…* one of the last frontiers in the 21st Century. I wish you many enlightened moments as we power-up and Mustang our way through time, life's story and your story.

'MASTERING THE MECHANICS OF YOUR LIFE' A ONE-ON-ONE COURSE FOR HEROES

Class Coordinator to The Team: "I believe *'The Mastering Course'* is a world first. To make sure it stays #1, we need to find new ways to improve our already pace-setting course for Heroes.

Usually, we (Child, Teenager and Maturing Adult) sit in my office/ classroom or an on-line Zoom-type consultation with the Course participant, our Hero, don't we? Lately, I've been thinking… I drive a mighty Mustang GT, why waste it sitting in a boring, unimaginative office/classroom? GT stands for Grand Tourer. Why not go on a road trip into time and find out firsthand why we were programmed and how life's survival story relates to our lives today. Admittedly, it may be a bit squashy for the three of you sitting in the backseat.

Then we can Fast Forward into the 21st Century with this information and stop at Childhood, Teenage and 'Maturing Adult' signposts to reconcile how life's survival programs are impacting each stage of our Hero's life today. What's the consensus? (Everyone smiling and nodding excitedly). Great! The Mustang is filled with high-octane fuel and ready to go.

We'll need plenty of supplies like water and snacks. Thinking trail- mix for the mighty Mustang journey into time; picnic type food for when we're back in the 21st Century. Team, can I rely on you to organise this? You know where the petty cash is kept. Thank you.

Teen, throw a footy into the boot and put some crayons, a colouring-in book and a blank drawing book for Child in the backseat please.

Clock's ticking… we've got an hour before our next Hero arrives and our new, improved Course starts. I'll get the paperwork ready for our new Hero to sign.

Let's make our Course for Heroes truly memorable and the best so far."

CAST OF CHARACTERS

Driver   The Course Coordinator, author and commentator, linking conversations and adding additional information, when required.

'Hero'   Appearing as You, the 'stuck', powerless and frustrated adult.

The three co-passengers/mentors/'backseat drivers':

Child   Appearing as You, the innocent 'inner child'
                      or
                      The Dictator of your life?

Teenager   Appearing as You, the dependent, compliant teen
                      or
                      The Rebellious Teenager?

Maturing Adult   Appearing as You, the powerless, conforming adult
                      or
                      The 'Midlife Crisis' delinquent maturing adult? ☺

THE GIST: AN EMPOWERING RIDE THROUGH TIME

Driver: "Let's welcome our new course Hero. (Everyone happily saying hello).

I'm your course commentator. We've got an amazing story to tell you! **Consciousness is the beginning of intellectual involvement with your life.** We love to watch our course heroes' breakthroughs! As well as your mentors, we are your cheer squad!

Congratulations on choosing our premium 'Life Education' Course. *'Mastering the Mechanics of your life,'* our one-on-one Course for heroes, is a toolbox for your intellectual and emotional intelligence and high-octane fuel for your journey into self-discovery and the treasure hunt for *your* personal power.

We've made big changes to our Course today. Instead of sitting in the usual classroom situation, we will be physically reversing through time in my mighty Mustang GT to the origins of life to learn about the survival system we inherited. We are all very excited at the idea. You can call me Driver. Can we call you Hero?"

Hero: *"Hello. I'm no hero. I'm just frustrated! But yes, you can call me 'Hero'."*

Driver: "First, please tell us why you are here today."

Hero: *"I'm the eldest of three siblings. Since I was a little kid, my parents always put me in charge of the other two. I somehow interpreted responsibility as a kind of power. I've never had much trouble accepting responsibility and taking the initiative, but lately I've been feeling 'stuck' and powerless, even doubting myself. Why is this happening?*

- *I've done everything I was taught to do...*

- *Everything I was supposed to do, should do, must do...*

- *I've lived by all the rules and all the standards...*

- *I trusted and believed this is the way life works...*

Why do I feel 'stuck' and powerless at my age and where is all my self-doubt coming from? Even taking responsibility for everything happening in my life, I'm not progressing? Why is my life in such a mess?!"

Driver: "Yep! Seems us humans need plenty of pain and lots of scar tissue before we start to heroically question our lives.

We also like to ask our Course Heroes to give us an understanding of their goal. Do you have a goal Hero?"

Hero: *"Yes. Basically, my goal is to understand where my feelings of 'stuckness' and powerlessness are coming from and what I can do about them. Anything more would be a bonus."*

Driver: "I assure you; we always aim higher than just achieving our Hero's goal.

I have another question for you Hero: where do you think your feelings of 'stuckness' and powerlessness are coming from?" (Hero takes a while to respond).

Hero: *"From sometime in my past, I guess."*

Driver: "You guessed right! From sometime in your past... mostly from your childhood to be exact.

What you learnt and were taught in childhood was probably generationally and generally correct at the time. But time changes everything! What's different today Hero from the time you were born and conditioned to all the rules, standards and expectations?"

Hero: *"Just about everything!"*

Driver: "Yes. Just about everything has changed since you were a child! Have you updated any beliefs or behaviours you learnt in your childhood or teenage years?"

Hero: *"No! Why would I? How are they relevant to what's happening in my life today? I don't remember any beliefs from my childhood, so how can I change them? Unreal question!"*

Driver: "Did anyone tell you that what you learnt in your formative years are repeated as present time responses in your adult life? That's right! You are living in a two-time zone system, designed for survival."

Hero: *"No way! (Shaking his head.) A child dictating my life? You can't be serious!"*

Driver: "Let me assure you Hero, understanding 'The survival system' you were born into will change your life. It takes courage to be in one of our Courses, especially *'The Mastering Course'.* Congratulations! You are already our Hero! Hold the two-time zone thought Hero; you'll soon see how and why this was a large and important part of our survival.

Now… we want you to know, you are safe with us. We are all basically your mentors, all here to help you understand your life from *a survival perspective* and the programs that helped us survive for thousands of years.

Would you like to put your baggage in the boot?"

Hero: *"What! How do you know I've got baggage? It's not on display!"*

Driver: "Trust me! Your baggage is always on display. Everyone brings their baggage to this Course, mostly from childhood. Basically, that's why you are here. We'll sort that out when we're back in the 21ˢᵗ Century. Child and Teenager will be particularly helpful in this area.

Now I'd like to introduce you to yourself at different ages and stages of your life. Your mirror-images are your 'backseat drivers' in many ways. They will be your mentors helping to explain and answer your questions and to make sense of how survival programs are impacting each stage of your life today.

First, meet Child. 'Child' is seven years old and represents you in the first seven years of your life. This relationship and its connection to the adult is known as your *inner child*… don't be fooled! Child has most of the answers to your current feelings of 'stuckness' and powerlessness and will help you understand how and why your childhood has everything to do with all stages of your life.

Denial that our childhood has anything to do with our current age or stage in life keeps most people living all their lives feeling powerless – angry with themselves and angry with life, wondering why their lives aren't working!"

Hero: *"Hello Child. It's nice to meet you. Are you really me? You are so young and cute!"*

Hero whispering to Driver: *"OMG! I am so turned off by the term 'inner child'. I can think for myself! I hope I'm not wasting my time... and money!"*

Driver: "Thank you Child. Let's assure Hero, that when he understands life's survival story, he'll be surprised to learn how much his childhood is involved in his life."

Child: "I love surprises!"

Driver: "We know you love surprises, Child. But your surprises are usually happy surprises. Hero has different kinds of surprises."

Hero: *"I look forward to your explanation... sounds like fairytale BS to me!"*

Driver: "Understood. Now meet yourself as a teenager. What do you think? How do you remember this time in your life? Disruptive? Bit of a blur? Don't worry, there's heaps to learn about this time zone and how it continues affecting you in your adult life."

Hero: *"Hello Teenager. I like your hair! I remember my teen years as being a bit chaotic, confusing... maybe. Still affecting me today? I doubt it. I grew out of that stage years ago."*

Teenager: "So that's what I look like at 40! Going grey already! It's my job to crank up your old memory Hero and give you the heads up on the teen time zone. It'll be an attitude changer!"

Driver: "Okay teen. It's *your* attitude I'll be watching! Harking back to your point Hero...

Most people think each stage of their lives are unrelated to previous stages – that they have outgrown the previous stage.

In fact, each stage is connected and builds on the previous stage/s as an aggregate total. Just like your childhood, the teenage time zone has major life forces stunting your potential as you mature.

Now I'd like to introduce you to yourself, the Maturing Adult and the much maligned and ridiculed 'Midlife Crisis' time zone. Say hello to your maturing self."

Hero: *"Hello! Nice to meet you. You look like me with a few wrinkles! Do I have a midlife crisis? Struth! That's the last thing I need! It would be seriously humiliating to be called out as having a midlife crisis! Should I be concerned?"*

Maturing Adult: "There's no need to worry. My explanation will help you understand what's really happening in this time zone."

Driver: "Questions? Anyone? No? Hero, I have some paperwork for you to sign before we leave…

Now, it's time to hop into the mighty Mustang. Would the three mentors settle into the rear passenger seats. You are in every way 'our' backseat drivers. Hero, sit in the front passenger seat next to me. Would someone hand out some bottles of water please. Remember to fasten your seatbelts.

Here's a Course journal and a pen Hero. You may like to jot down your thoughts and any important realisations.

Let's change the programs running in Hero's head Team and investigate the many levels of his 'stuckness' and powerlessness.

Not sure what time we'll be back in the 21st Century…"

SECTION I:

REVERSING INTO
CAVEMAN TIMES

PRIMITIVE SURVIVAL AND OUR PROGRAMMED LIVES

Driver: "Hear the unmistakable sound and tone of the big Mustang V8 engine? Sounds like love to me! ☺ Even in reverse and all the weight it's carrying, you can still feel its power, can't you! Lives up to its reputation – a muscle car!"

Maturing Adult: "I've seen this car in the parking lot. I didn't know it was yours. It's a modern version, isn't it? Why didn't you buy one of the original models from the 1960s or 70s, or better, a Shelby?"

Driver: "I was never really into cars until I saw the 2017 model. I knew I had to park one in my garage."

Teenager: "Have you named it? Everyone names their cars."

Driver: "I call it 'The Legend'."

Teenager: "Perfect name. It is a Legend, isn't it? Steve McQueen in the movie Bullitt and all the stories about Carroll Shelby and later when he joined forces with Ford. Hello Legend."

Driver: "Oh! Your knowledge of 'The Legend' is impressive Teen. First time in a mighty Mustang? Enjoy your ride…"

Child: "Are we there yet?"

Driver: "Not yet sweet child. We're just getting started. It will take some time. We are travelling back through thousands of years. Would you like to play 'I spy' with your backseat companions while I explain a few more things to our new Hero?"

Child: "I love I spy! Can I start?"

Driver: "Yes, you can start.

Some basic information for you Hero. In caveman times – the hunters and gatherers, life was nothing more than survival. It's a hostile and dangerous place with dinosaurs, brontosaurus T-rex's, sabre-toothed tigers and the like roaming the countryside, looking for their next meal. Belonging to and conforming with 'The Pack' were an integral part of caveman survival. It meant protection, safety in numbers and security etc.

We're still a few hours away from our destination Hero. To fill in some time, would you like to join in with your backseat drivers and play 'I spy'?"

Hero: *"Sure. What's the clue?"*

***

Driver: "We've now reached our destination. To help you feel a little more at ease, because we reversed into time, the Mustang is now facing the exit. I'll leave the engine running just in case we need a fast getaway! Please stay in the car and be on the lookout for any tribes or large animals. We don't know how they'll react if they see us!

Child, Teenager has your crayons and your colouring-in and drawing books ready for you. Please sit quietly while we're here. We don't want to disturb anything in this time zone, do we? (Child shaking his head).

Let's find a cave. Entrances to the caves were camouflaged behind lots of greenery etc. to help our primitive cousins survive. There's an entrance… (pointing). Everyone be on the lookout for any signs of movement.

Ready to learn about survival programs, Hero? Your understanding of life in the 21ˢᵗ Century is about to change, forever!"

Hero: *Nodding. "I hadn't thought about life beginning way back in time... in some cave! I don't see the connection! It's a scary place, isn't it?"*

Driver: "Sure is:

- Back then, to help us survive without a thinking brain, we lived instinctively and reactively. You could say a knee-jerk way of reacting to life – no thinking!

- We didn't have a language. Our communication with each other was physical and emotional, using gestures, nods and grunts. Children copied the tribes' behaviours.

- We lived a very short lifespan, somewhere between 20 and 35 years.

'The system' and its non-intellectual programs were about survival and nothing more."

Hero: *"When you say survival, what do you mean, exactly?"*

Driver: "Good question:

- Survival is basically eat, drink, sleep, procreate... repeat.

- Copying behaviours handed down from one generation to the next.

- No thinking required."

Hero: *"What kind of survival programs are you talking about?"*

Driver:

- "We were all born with a Will to Survive. Our self-protective instincts, feelings and senses were all operating and geared to survival.

- The Will to Survive translated into a 'Need to belong' to the tribe, to be cared for, safe and protected.

- Abandonment was a primal fear. How will we survive?

- 'Belonging' to the tribe was the difference between life and death. 'The tribe' and its conforming mentality helped us survive and maintained order. All species of life have a need to belong to their kind e.g., schools of fish, herds of sheep, packs of wolves etc. 'The group' helped us survive.

- Fear was built into our DNA. We lived in its safe comfort zones, intuitively on-alert to its silent warnings. Again, all about survival.

- 'Fight or flight' reactions to fear helped our primitive cousins escape danger and survive.

- Sexual/primal urges throughout our lives ensured the survival of all species.

All those programs are still operating today. Who can change them, advance them or switch them off?

The big questions for me when I started my research into time, was why we repeat generational cycles and how did we survive without a thinking brain? Turns out, this is a major key to understanding life today:

- The subconscious mind was our primitive survival memory.

- What the child saw frequently, he copied. Those copied behaviours were hardwired into a child's subconscious mind as basic survival memories.

- Subconscious survival memories repeating generational cycles became our fast, automatic way of *reacting* to life, helping us survive for thousands of years.

Two time zones, one reaction.

Basic survival behaviours learnt in childhood are automatically repeated in present time as a present time reaction!

Generational cycles mindlessly repeating themselves.

No thinking! Fast, automatic, kneejerk subconscious reactions = survival."

Hero: *"Are you saying we have no say in our subconscious reactions?"*

Driver: "No, I'm saying, if we deny or have no knowledge of the two time zones operating in our lives in the 21ˢᵗ Century, then we continue *reacting* to life via our subconscious hardwired childhood survival beliefs and copied generational behaviours, eventually feeling 'stuck' and powerless as maturing adults living in the child's time zone."

Hero: *"So when I react rather than think then respond to my current situation, I'm living in the caveman reactive survival system."*

Driver: "That's right! Fascinating, isn't it! Subconscious reactions helped us survive. No thinking! I call them kneejerk reactions. Reacting kept us alive when we couldn't think! Today, your subconscious is responsible for around 90 – 95% of your automatic reactions to what is happening in your life in present time.

Another way to put it: the sophisticated hi-tech world of the 21st Century is being upstaged by subconscious survival intelligence!

When your subconscious recognises a situation from the past that is like what is happening in present time, *it reacts.* You know exactly what to do, how you feel, how to behave… without thinking. It's our reactive way of surviving. Two different time zones i.e., past and present… one reaction. Those ingenious survival programs have helped us survive for thousands of years."

Hero: *"You are making sense. I'm trying to work out how it's affecting me today."*

Driver: "Great! Have you heard of Aristotle? He was an Ancient Greek philosopher 384 B.C. – 322 B.C. and is well known for his famous quote:

"Give me a child until he is seven and I will show you the man."

In other words, the adult repeats his learnt childhood beliefs and copied generational behaviours as a present time response. Generational cycles mindlessly and robotically repeating themselves – caveman stuff!"

Hero: *"🔔🔔🔔 'Ah-ha' Now I'm beginning to understand why I feel so 'stuck' and powerless at my age! If I'm unconsciously repeating my beliefs from childhood and the generational behaviours I copied, then I'm the classic child in Aristotle's quote!"*

Driver whispering: "Guys! Hero just had his first 'ah-ha' moment! We love breakthroughs into Higher consciousness. This is what our Courses are all about! We'll cheer loudly when we are safely away from here!

Back to you Hero. The survival system and its programs haven't changed, nor have they advanced. Who can switch them off or upgrade them? It bears repeating: childhood beliefs and copied generational behaviours learnt in the first seven years become our automatic reactions to life, potentially for the rest of our lives. For example, if a child regularly witnesses Domestic Violence, he deems it to be 'normal' behaviour and repeats that 'normal' behaviour to his own family years later. Scary stuff, isn't it? Again, no thinking... just fast reactive behaviours repeating copied generational behaviours from an earlier time zone."

Hero: *"Are you saying everyone is on autopilot? The same as cavemen, when we had no working intellectual brain?"*

Driver: "Yes! Until we, as adults, realise we are r*eacting rather than responding* to current circumstances, the survival system we were born into remains in charge – no matter our age, stage or status."

Hero: *"How do I know if I'm reacting or responding?"*

Driver: "If you're not thinking through and considering your options to your current circumstances, then you are *reacting* subconsciously. You don't have to remember your childhood beliefs, attitudes or your behaviours because they are immediately on display via your kneejerk reaction to your present situation, whatever that is."

Teenager whispering: "Sush! Over there! Can you see a small group of females and a few children running around? Are they fossicking for berries and herbs? Can they hear the Mustang idling?"

Driver whispering: "Yes, they are the gatherers. The Mustang is quiet on idle. We'll be okay. It's the giant animals from this primitive era that we need to fear. The females will most likely run if they see us. Ah! They've turned and now they're walking towards the entrance to their cave. The men and the boys are probably out hunting, hoping to bring back a small animal they've speared or trapped to cook as part of tonight's dinner.

In case you are wondering, becoming pregnant in their early teens and having three to four children, two or three surviving, seems to be the consensus. As there's no documented evidence, we can only presume to know. Sounds about right though, doesn't it? No contraceptives back then. A tough life without anaesthetics, too."

Hero: *"There must be some changes in thousands of years. I know we are living a much longer lifespan today. Are there any other changes?"*

Driver: "Yes. We *are* living two, three, even four times longer than our primitive cousins. Today our intellectual brain is operating and evolving and 'The individual' is slowly emerging, particularly in midlife.

I'd like to point out: 'The system' we were born into gave its power to 'The Pack' and its conforming mentality. Survival was about belonging to the pack/the tribe with its safety in numbers, protecting the individual, helping us survive. Today 'The Pack' is the family, our generation, the status quo – the groups' conforming mentality."

Maturing Adult: "By our age, Hero, we've outlived the survival system and we've outgrown our conditioning."

Hero: *"Why don't we know this? It's so basic!"*

Driver whispering: Like I said earlier Hero, most people have difficulty accepting the 'inner child' concept and the two time zones of 'The system'. I simply wait 'til they are in so much pain they start making enquiries about our Courses. Sobering, isn't it?"

Hero: *"Just like I was hurting and so frustrated with my life?"*

Driver: "Exactly. Any more questions Hero?"

Hero: *"All good for now."*

Teenager: "This place is freaking me out! Lucky, we didn't see a dinosaur! Let's get out of here fast! Giddy up Pony!"

Driver: "Yes, let's Fast Forward into the 21st Century. I've engaged 'Sports Mode' but it will still take a while. Water, snacks anyone? Who's in charge of snacks?

We owe Hero a hip, hip for his lightbulb moment in the caveman time zone."

Child: "Can I say hip, hip first?"

Driver: "Yes. As loud as you can. This is a celebration into Higher consciousness. Let's cheer Hero on."

Child: "Hip, hip for Hero. Are we there yet?"

Driver: "Not yet darling Child. Are you feeling a little sleepy? It's been a big day so far and we're just getting started."

Child: "A little bit. Will you wake me up when we get to the picnic ground?"

Teenager: "I'll give you an elbow when we get there Child."

Driver: "You mean a gentle nudge, Teen!"

Teenager: "Whatever!"

Driver: "Hero, here's a couple of quotes to align you with the 21st Century:

The late Dr. Stephen Hawking, 1942-2018, the English theoretical physicist, cosmologist and author once said:

"We are just an advanced breed of monkeys on a minor planet of a very average star. But we can understand the Universe. That makes us something very special."

The late Dr. Carl Yung, 1875-1961, Swiss psychiatrist and psychoanalyst, author, illustrator, correspondent and founder of the term 'inner child' once said:

"Until you make your unconscious conscious, it will direct your life and you will call it fate."

And, to help you understand the power of your subconscious mind, Hero, we've compiled a couple of Handouts for you to take home. That's how important the subconscious mind is in our lives, even today."

Hero: *"Thank you. I've got a few more notes to write before I take a nap too."*

Driver: "I'll wake everyone when we get back. The mighty Mustang will need petrol."

Hero's notes:

....

....

....

....

....

....

....

....

....

....

....

....

....

....

....

....

....

....

....

SECTION II:

FAST FORWARD INTO THE 21ST CENTURY

CHILDHOOD SIGNPOST

Driver: "Wakey! Wakey! It's been a few hours. We're just coming into the 21st Century now. I can see the 'Childhood' signpost from here.

Please be on the lookout for a petrol station. There's one already! I'll only be a minute.

Back in the mighty Mustang. From now on guys, when I pull over, it's safe to get out of the car. This picnic ground looks good, doesn't it? Plenty of seating and there's a playground and toilet facilities. Let's stretch our legs, shall we?

Perfect timing for a late lunch. Who's hungry? The Team put a picnic lunch together for us before you arrived Hero. Let's see what's in the basket. Looks delicious! Yum! Sandwiches, juice, small cakes and fruit! You've excelled Team. Thank you. Let's relax for a while and enjoy our picnic in the sun…"

***

Driver: "Okay, back to business.

Child, please stay in my sight. Don't go running off! We need you to help make sense of Hero's life, very soon."

Child: "Okay. I'll be over there (pointing) playing footy with Teen."

Driver: "Hero, as referenced earlier, viewing your childhood as a temporary learning experience introduces a powerful new perspective to the adult's position."

Hero: *"How and when in the first seven years does the survival system come into play?"*

Driver: "From the moment we were born. Some say earlier, but let's agree with the moment we were born. It all starts with the tribal family. First, we are all born different. Even the sequence of our birth sets us up for different experiences. For instance, the first child usually bears more responsibility than say, the second or third child."

Hero: *"Like me! I was the eldest and responsible for my brother and sister."*

Driver: "Yep! That's how it usually works.

(Driver calling out to Child). Your turn Child. Please give Hero an understanding of yourself and the first seven years."

Child: "Hi. I was born with a Will to Survive. My self-protective instincts, senses and feelings were operating. Fear kept me safe in my comfort zones. I'm a literal child which means I view everything at face value. I trust my instincts; I pick-up on attitudes and I copy repeated behaviours from my tribal family and important others. Everything I see, hear and feel frequently in the first seven years, I store as a survival memory. My thinking brain is in its simple stages and can't question, discriminate or reason *or help me to survive.*"

Driver: "Thank you Child. You did a wonderful job of explaining your part in Hero's life."

Child: "And I did it all by myself."

Driver: "Oh! Yes, you did! You explained your story all by yourself and you put your survival beliefs and copied behaviours together, without being asked, all by yourself too. You're our little star and you deserve a star! In fact, you deserve two stars ★★ You are so important to us, not just in childhood, but throughout our lives. Child, I'll add a little more detail for Hero now. Please stay with us."

Hero interjecting: *"That was a really clear explanation. Thank you, Child. I do have one question: Why do little kids ask 'why' if, as you say, they can't question?"*

Driver: "Great question Hero. Little kids around the ages of 3 – 4 years old do ask 'why' frequently, don't they? Generally, their why questions are not questioning or disputing what we say, rather it's a basic question like, *'where do rainbows come from?'* showing their curiosity as their intellectual brain is developing. How much they understand our explanation... is the real question."

Hero: *"Of course, 'why' is simple; comprehending the explanation, especially a complex explanation, requires more intellectual development."*

Maturing Adult interjecting: "Struth! We can't answer our own questions half the time let alone answer their 'why' questions!" ☺

Driver: "True. Hero, do you know your childhood survival foundations are known as the 'Childhood Model'? A blueprint for how life works, how life is supposed to be, forever... according to a literal, powerless child."

Hero: *"Now I'm curious. I've never heard of the 'Childhood Model'. What kind of things would be in the Model?"*

Driver: "The 'Childhood Model' contains such things as:

- Generational themes, values and attitudes.

- A need to belong – to survive.

- Everything we observed, heard and felt frequently.

- Copied and coping behaviours like staying out of the spotlight, blaming, avoidance etc.

- A need to fit in and conform.

- Fear and comfort zone boundaries.

- Little, if any, reference to time and change.

- Standards, rules, controls and limitations.

- Should, should not, must and supposed to beliefs and behaviours.

- No responsibility for himself.

- No alternative choices – we lived in an either/or world of yes-or-no, right-or-wrong, can-or can't.

- Feelings of powerlessness.

- No independence.

- A serious, personal world with no humour about himself.

- Images and beliefs about himself, formed from the opinions of others.

Hero, can you think of any others?"

Hero: *"Not off the top of my head. I didn't know this!* 😔😔😔 *This is a revelation to me! I had no idea. So much I'm learning today! Thank you. You've already changed my understanding of life."*

Driver: "Another dawning moment for Hero, Team. And we are just getting started. Congratulations Hero! You are taking this information like a duck to water! We love working with you too. Say a big cheer for Hero guys! ☺☺☺☺

The Childhood Model's crude survival beliefs and copied behaviours and the two time zones with their *subconscious kneejerk reactions* continue operating throughout our lives, even after we wise-up!

Remember we were not meant to live longer than 35 years. I also make the point: our literal childhood beliefs are very outdated and *emotionally constricting* by the time we reach the Maturing Adult stage today.

Living in Childhood Model constraints will always leave the adult with feelings of self-doubt, 'not enough', compromised, 'stuck' and powerless. The beliefs in the Model are known colloquially as 'childhood baggage' (the baggage you put in the boot earlier Hero). We now know how and why childhood hardwired beliefs and copied behaviours learnt in the first seven years, with the two time zones operating, becomes our baggage. Powerful knowledge today!"

Hero: *"OMG! 🔔🔔🔔 Now I really get it! I've been unconsciously repeating the stuff I learnt in my formative years. You've already achieved my goal!!!"*

Driver: "Guys! Another lightbulb moment for Hero! We've achieved Hero's goal already! Three cheers for Hero and the Team! ☺☺☺☺

The reasons why we deny the concept of the 'inner child', let alone its power is basically because:

- Our ego and intellectual brain have difficulty accepting that a child under seven years old is directing our lives.

- Generally, we are not conscious of our fast, subconscious subliminal reactions – nor are we aware that our survival attitudes, beliefs and behaviours are already formed, no thinking required.

- Our survival instincts and survival beliefs in our Childhood Model don't like to be tampered with.

- And the big one, when we don't understand the survival system and it's two time zone, one reaction program."

Hero: *"Of course.* 💡💡💡 *It's almost like 'The system' is ganging-up against the individual ever becoming equal to or more powerful than 'The Group' and 'The survival system' combined, isn't it?"*

Driver: "Another win for Hero and the 21ˢᵗ Century. Hooray for Hero. Four lightbulbs now. Well done Hero! You are such an inspiration! ☺☺☺☺

Ganging-up. I've never thought of it that way. Interesting take, Hero. To help you stay convinced and connected, think about this:

On what do we base our lives, if not our childhood?

- Where do our feelings about ourselves and 'not enough' come from?

- Where do our beliefs, comfort zones, behaviours etc. come from?

- Where do our fears come from? e.g., fear of change.

- Where else but childhood did we learn to fit in and conform?"

Hero: *"That consolidates it! Can you give me some examples of the differences between childhood and adult time zones?"*

Driver: "I'd like you to meet your Teenager time zone first otherwise some of the examples won't give you the full story. In the meantime, what if Child explains his perspective on different subjects in the Childhood Model? You'll get the gist immediately and know where your feelings of powerlessness are coming from today. No offence Child."

Child: "It's okay. I'm little and I have no power."

Hero: *"Great idea Driver. From all accounts Child, you have lots of power! A lot more than 'we' give you credit for!"*

Driver: "The little kid in you has no idea of its importance in your life. He sees himself as an innocent, powerless child but... when you add your survival programming, he is potentially *'The Dictator of Your Life'!* How you were treated as a child and your childhood beliefs about yourself, often interpreted from important others' comments, can be a BIG reason why we are held back and never fulfill our potential. The early years are critical to the whole of our lives."

Child: "Can I give you my example now?"

Driver and Hero in unison: "Yes please."

Child: "When people call me names or tell me I'm stupid, I feel ashamed and I believe them because I can't question, discriminate or reason. I'm literal and I trust what I hear, see and feel at face value. I accept their words and I hate myself for being stupid. Sometimes I cry. 'Stupid' makes me feel bad and sad. I try hard to get everything right. There's lots to learn everyday and some days I'm tired. I try to fit in and make everyone proud of me. 'Stupid' impacts my self-esteem and my self-worth, where my sense of deserving comes from."

Hero: *"I've never thought of it like that before Child! Of course! So, the people who call you stupid or similar names are seeing you at their intellectual level and generally not seeing your age group through its simple, non-intellectual, literal position. Is that right? And you might be tired when you're learning every day. I know I get tired without a break."*

Child: "Yes. It's not fair. I can't explain, I just feel the pain. Some people think when I don't understand words that I won't understand what they're saying about me. But kids are born instinctual and we know a lot by the tone in people's voices and their facial expressions… even when they are happy to see us or not and we sense their attitudes too."

Hero: *"That's very clever, Child. I won't forget that! Now I really 'get the concept'. Child, can you give me more examples of how you interpret subjects in your Childhood Model?"*

Driver interjecting: "I'd like to assure you Hero, from personal experience, some of your childhood beliefs will die hard! Hardwired and attached to survival, letting go of a belief, especially one you *want* to believe, can be a difficult and painful experience. (Whispering… like learning about Father Christmas!) It's one of the hardest things you will need to do if a belief is holding you back or not working in your best interests today."

Child (to driver): "Can I share more?"

Driver: "Yes, go ahead Child."

Child: "My **'Need to belong'** is the most basic one. My will to survive translated into my need to belong. My survival depends on someone caring for me. I'm totally dependent on my carers in every way. Abandonment is my greatest fear – it's a primal fear. How will I survive without my carers?"

Hero: *"🔔🔔🔔 Ah-ha! It's easy to see how basic the survival system really is... like an unconscious memory that drives us to belong, conforming with the group for survival reasons. Now, as I mature, I'll think of belonging as a choice. Thank you, Child. Any more wisdom?"*

Driver interjecting: "Another 'ah-ha' for Hero everyone! Hooray! Cheers Hero. We love your breakthroughs into consciousness. Five now, if I'm counting correctly! Three cheers for Hero! ☺☺☺☺

We're just tipping the iceberg on belonging issues and there's lots more in the Teenage time zone. Go ahead Child, please."

Child: "**Time and change.** I have no understanding of time. I live in a 'now' world. I don't like change because it makes me feel confused and frightened. I want everything to stay the same and fear makes me stay in my comfort zones."

Hero: *"OMG! 🔔🔔🔔 Now your fear of change is coming through to me as my negative reactions to change! This is making so much sense! Thank you so much Child."*

Driver: "Another lightbulb for Hero, Team! Cheers Hero. You are definitely our #1 Hero. Hip, hip ☺☺☺☺"

23

Child: "Can I share some more?"

Driver: "Yes Child. You've got the spotlight."

Child: "**Generational attitudes:** I copy everyone who is close to me. Like I said before, I instinctively pick up their attitudes and their deep-seated beliefs and behaviours handed down from earlier generations, like gender roles and equality."

Hero: *"Now I understand why it can take several generations to change an attitude, sometimes even longer. It's so easy to understand how the world works when seen through our survival programming. Anymore?"*

Child: "**Choices:** I don't believe I have alternative choices. I live in an either/or world of yes-or-no, right-or-wrong, can-or-can't. There are no maybe's or grey areas in my world."

Hero: *"Ah-ha! 🔔🔔🔔 Of course! Your world is yes-or-no, isn't it! Now it's obvious why I feel 'stuck' in certain situations when I don't understand the either/or black-or-white world of my inner child. And, of course, I can now negotiate a better outcome for myself at my age too. Amazing, anymore?"*

Driver interjecting: "More ah-ha's for Hero Team. What a memorable day for our Hero! Cheers Hero! Hooray! ☺☺☺☺"

Maturing Adult interrupting: "Teen and I are going to kick the football for a while. We'll still hear what's happening and will join the cheering when Hero conquers another of his obstacles."

Teenager: "I'll show the old guy how to really play footy!"

Driver: "Okay. I'll call you when we need your input. Thanks guys. Enjoy! Your turn again, Child. Are you having fun?"

Child: "Yes. I'm having fun. I feel a little bit important."

Driver and Hero in unison: "You're very important!"

Child: "You'll like this one Hero. **Conformity:** I have to behave and conform or I'll get into trouble. Fear doesn't like me being called out or being different to the other kids. I obey fear. Conforming keeps me safe and I feel secure too."

Hero: "Oh! 🔔🔔🔔 *No wonder I find it difficult to break from the ranks and speak up! I never understood why I felt this way. Intimidating group pressure again and the survival need to belong and conform, isn't it? So survival based, so simple!"*

Driver: "More bells ringing for our Hero guys! Can you hear us Teen and Maturing Adult? Yes, that's great! Give Hero another hooray! We love hearing bells ring for our Heroes. ☺☺☺☺ Over to you again, Child."

Child: "**Feelings:** are my way of communicating… my emotional language. My carers communicate with me using words. When I'm little, I can't understand most of their words. It's hard to get them to understand me sometimes when we are communicating in different ways and on different levels."

Hero: *"Of course. You are making so much sense. Why aren't I aware of this? Can you give me an example of communicating emotionally, Child?"*

Child: "Yes. I can give you a simple example of communicating emotionally when I was much younger. It was the transition between non-verbal, when I used my feelings to express myself, before I started to use words. My carers sometimes called my frustration 'two-year-old tantrums'. They laughed at me and my behaviour, sometimes isolating me in a corner or in my bedroom until I calmed down. I needed a hug and reassurance that I was okay, that my frustration was temporary until I learned more words... not isolation! My situation was frustrating me... nothing to do with tantrums."

Hero: *"🔔🔔🔔 You must have been frustrated! You were communicating with us using your emotional language and we were speaking to you using our intellect and words. Calling it a two-year-old tantrum is really missing the point, isn't it? You were frustrated! So sorry! How about another couple of your literal ways of seeing your life/our life? The differences between the child and the adult time zones is making so much sense to me. Thank you."*

Driver: "Another breakthrough for Hero guys. This is amazing! We love how quickly you've caught on. A big cheer for our Hero! Hooray! ☺☺☺☺ Over to you again, Child."

Child: "Responsibility: I have no responsibility for myself. Everyone cared for me... I will always be dependent on others for everything. I live in my childhood model all my life. I will always feel dependent and powerless."

Hero: *"Oh, of course! 🔔🔔🔔 Taking ownership of my life is my responsibility at my age, not blaming or avoiding or feeling like I have no power. Not taking responsibility makes the maturing adult behave powerlessly or no offence, acting childishly! Wow! You're doing so well explaining yourself to me, kiddo. One more?"*

Driver: "Another breakthrough for Hero Team. You are now the Hero of our Course heroes. Three cheers for Hero! ☺☺☺☺ Do you have one more for Hero, Child?"

Child: "Yes. **My need to be perfect:** I try my hardest to get things right, to be good all the time and to make my carers proud of me. It's a kind of bargain I make with myself to please my carers and important others so I will be loved and cared for. It feels like I get a better response and more love from my carers when I please them and get everything right! Sometimes I believe I must be perfect to be loved."

Hero: *"😞😞😞 I will never see my childhood and you/us the same way again. This has been a huge wake-up for me… a revelation in many ways. I can't thank you enough my inner child!"*

Driver: "You are not going to believe this Team! Our Hero just described his inner child/adult relationship as a huge wake-up. You are amazing Hero! We love how easily this information has registered with you. Cheers Hero and cheers Team!" ☺☺☺☺

Hero: *"From my point of view, the two time zones and its ingenious way of surviving is the reason why, at my maturing stage, I feel so frustrated and:*

- *Why I have so many self-doubts.*

- *Why I fear change.*

- *Why I feel a 'need to belong'.*

- *Why I feel insecure and why I need certainty.*

- *Why I don't like feeling embarrassed, humiliated, put in the spotlight etc.*

- *Why I'm sometimes in conflict with myself.*

- *Why I hold myself back sometimes.*

- *Why I'm emotionally dependent on others to feel okay about myself.*

- *Why I sometimes think I have no alternative choices; that I can't or shouldn't negotiate a better deal or a better outcome for myself.*

- *Why I'm so serious and take myself and my life so seriously. And, why I have no humour about myself.* **Being a child is serious stuff, isn't it?**

- *Why I dislike myself.*

- *Why I feel I must be perfect to be loved.*

- *Why I recognise some of my behaviours and expressions are a repeat of my parents' behaviours and their expectations too.*

- *Why I feel intimidated and conform with group thinking rather than thinking for myself.*

- *Why love and acceptance from others has often been more important than self-love and self-acceptance.*

There are so many things working against me ever fulfilling my potential when I don't understand my connection with my childhood, my inner child, the two time zones and of course, the power of 'The group'! Love this Course!"

Driver: "We love your feedback Hero! You have summed up brilliantly why *you* are feeling 'stuck' and powerless in the two-time zone system we inherited.

One more thing: every child's childhood is unique to that child and contains a different set of experiences, beliefs and copied behaviours. Some of your examples of why you feel frustrated that you mentioned a minute ago will be different for everyone."

Hero: *"That makes sense. We are all different, but our lives are based on the same survival system. So, each person could question themselves from the subjects in the Childhood Model and work out which ones are most likely causing their frustration. Even better, they could enrol in this Course or read one of your books!"*

Driver: "Thank you, Hero. The Childhood Model, subconscious reactions and becoming aware of the two time zones are key."

Hero: *"Hey kiddo. Now I understand 'our' story, I want to tell you, you are now my Hero. Would you like to work with me? We can build our own dream-team. What do you think?"*

Child: "Will you take care of me? I will always live in my Childhood Model and my fear-based comfort zones. *I want to feel safe and secure all the time.* I'll be very anxious with anything I'm unfamiliar with, which means you'll feel anxious too. **Fear and my need to feel secure all the time will be bossing you around too, trying to keep you in my comfort zones."**

Hero: *"We are sooo connected. You see, I like to feel safe all the time too kiddo! Don't worry! I've got this! I understand 'us' now! We'll be fine; I'll keep you safe and protected. You give me your take on things that are happening in our life through my automatic subconscious reactions, and I'll intellectually respond with an outcome that works in our best interests today in 'real-time'. What do you say?"*

Child: "Sounds okay. If you want me to leave my comfort zones, you'll need to give me lots of encouragement."

Hero: *"Can I add further assurance to my inner child?"*

Driver: "Of course."

Hero: *"When I encourage you and give you confidence to move forward with me, I'm giving myself the encouragement and confidence I need to move forward too. I'll tell you, the frightened little kid in me, that 'we' are okay and you are safe with me. Will that help ease your anxiety?"*

Child: "A bit. But you'll have to get past my fear every time you want to expand my boundaries and build a bigger life."

Hero: *"It's okay, I've got this now. I can work with our survival programs! I'm seeing those programs as seriously super-protective. They are dumbing us down when we deny life's survival forces! Life's story really is our story, isn't it?"*

Driver: "Great job Child. Hero really understands your place in his life now and the survival principles. Let's give Hero and Child a big cheer! Want to do the hip, hips Child? Really, really, loudly this time."

Child: "Hip, hip… (shouting) and laughing" ☺

Driver: "Are you ready for the Teenage time zone, Hero? There's still lots more to learn about 'The group' and conforming and where more of your feelings of powerlessness are coming from today."

Hero: *"Yes, I'm ready for the next stage. I'll make a few notes on the way to the next signpost. I don't want to forget anything."*

Driver: "Okay. Let's quickly clean up, pack-up and throw our rubbish in the bins over there (pointing). Everyone back in the mighty Mustang. It won't take long to drive to the Teenage signpost, especially in Sports Mode. It's just a few clicks away. Let's get you in the mood Teen. Fancy some Hip Hop/Rap or how about some Heavy Metal? Nothing like Heavy Metal… perfect music for the mighty Mustang!"

Hero's notes:

....

....

....

....

....

....

....

....

....

....

....

....

....

....

....

....

....

....

TEENAGE SIGNPOST

Driver: "The Teenage signpost is coming into view now. We'll pull in here. Another great park with plenty of space. Let's alight. More water anyone?

This looks like the best table and seating to take in the wider view. What do you think? Enough room? Child, would you like to sit with us and use your crayons to draw us something while Teen helps Hero understand his time zone?"

Child: "I'll draw us having a picnic."

Driver: "Sounds interesting. We'll look forward to seeing it later.

Hero, I should explain a couple of things. First, there was no such thing as a teenager in primitive times. With such a short lifespan and without an evolving intellectual brain, life hadn't been dissected and categorised into stages like we do today.

As teenagers in caveman times, you probably would've been a parent, maybe twice, even three times. That's a scary thought, isn't it? And another big difference, you would not have ventured away from the tribe.

All the survival forces that governed your childhood, govern the Teenager:

- You continue to live in the two time zone system.

- The survival foundations in your Childhood Model are now 'on-file' in your subconscious mind waiting to react to a belief, behaviour or attitude that is happening in present time.

- No thinking required, just automatically reacting.

- A programmed need to belong and conform with 'The group' continues:

Every child wants to fit-in and blend in with their friends.

Teenagers want to assimilate and blend in with their peer group.

'Different' is a difficult fit in these two stages.

How are you going with this, Hero?"

Hero: *"Taking it all in, thanks."*

Driver: "Good. Just like babies born into a new, scary and often confusing world, teenagers are thrown into this new, scary and often confusing stage, with little experience or understanding of how to manage the many complexities of their evolving lives. Transition is always disruptive – no matter our age, stage or status in life.

Hero, what's the first word that comes to mind when you think of teenagers?"

Hero: *"I automatically think of teens and rebellion."*

Teenager: "Great! That word again. So superficial! It's a joke! It annoys the crap out of me that people don't look deeper and see what we are really trying to do and what we're up against with our limited life experience."

Driver: "Okay teen, settle down. You're right Hero. Most people automatically think of teenagers and rebellion together. Even parents admit they dread the time when their children become teenagers. That's how endemic the thinking is about teenagers and rebellion. They generally don't see the depth of this transitioning time zone. We'll change that! Hero won't be thinking of teens as only rebellious when you and I explain your teen story. Okay?"

Teenager: "Okay. The word 'rebellious' lights me up!"

Driver: "Got it! Hang on Teen, your turn soon. Now, where were we? Oh yes! Let me set the scene so Hero can relate more easily to your story.

Today the teenage time zone is a major transitioning time in our lives. We are no longer a child. We are growing up! Teens are pulling away, a little bit and pushing some of the boundaries of the tribal family rules and childhood conformity. They are forming an important new alliance with their peer group, the next generation, to run the show. This new alliance exerts enormous pressure to conform so they'll be accepted and supported by 'The group'. The group, once again, rules! Teen can explain more in a minute."

Teen interjecting: "We really have no independence, at all. We are just moving the goal posts from one set of rules to the next... often harsher rules."

Hero: *"I've never thought of it quite like that before. So, the Teen time zone is seen by adults as rebellious, but for teenagers, it's about pushing against their childhood boundaries a little bit, in line with their need for some independence and their continuing development. At the same time, they are forming a new alliance with their generation for acceptance. So less about survival with the tribe and more about acceptance by their generation. Have I got this right?"*

Driver: "Yes and I add here, fear of rejection by their peer group is the greatest fear in the Teenage time zone."

Hero: *"So, fear of rejection is now replacing our childhood fear of abandonment? I do remember some pressure to fit in, but I also wanted to be accepted. Do we ever feel powerful? I mean, do we ever get our freedom?"*

Teenager interjecting: "Not in my stage, you don't!"

Hero: *"So, teenagers are separating from the tribal family and forming a new alliance with their generation. Just thinking… it would be a scary place if a teen felt he didn't fit in anywhere. Separating from his tribal family and not being accepted by his peer group and having no financial means to support himself would be pretty terrifying, wouldn't it? And social media would be adding more pressure as well. Suddenly I see a different, more serious side to the teen transitioning zone. Love this. Go on…"*

Driver: "Good. Remember, 'The survival system' empowered 'The Pack'. The group and its conforming mentality rules! If you belong to a group, you are expected to conform with its rules. That's the way 'The system' works. **The group, whoever they are, will always appear to be more powerful than the individual.**"

Hero: *"You have no idea how much this is making sense to me! Another breakthrough! 🔔🔔🔔 Thank you everyone!"*

Driver: "Another breakthrough for Hero team! Well done Hero. We love your grasp on this. Three cheers for Hero! ☺☺☺☺

Hey Teen, want to take Hero behind the scenes?"

Teenager: "Sure. I want to start by saying, the act of separating from tribal authority figures is not personal! We're not trying to upset anyone, but our change in appearance, behaviour and attitude makes us appear rebellious. No doubt the term 'rebellious' was coined by 'The Establishment' because from their point of view, that is how teens' sometimes loud, aggressive, non-conforming behaviours appear. Just surface stuff!

I'd like to add some powerful, often overlooked themes in the Teenage time zone. Here's a two-pronged issue to begin:

First, we are developing physically, so we look more grown up. Some adults and teachers see us as physically closer in size to them and then mistakenly presume we can think like adults too.

Here's the thing: adults generally don't realise that our intellectual brain is a work-in-progress in our adolescent and teen years and is restructuring and rewiring itself. Physically we may look more like an adult but our intellectual brain hasn't kept pace with our physical development. Our intellectual brain continues its development until we are about 25-years old." *

Hero: *"Oh! I didn't know that! This shines new light on the teenage perspective, doesn't it? What does the intellectual brain restructure and rewire?"*

Teenager: "It begins with physical co-ordination and motor skills in adolescence and early teens, then emotional reactions in mid-teens and finally 'judgements and control' begin around 21 years through to 25 years."

Hero: *"Just curious… can you give me an example?"*

Teenager: "Sure. * The Dunedin Study, New Zealand, found that teenage offending is the norm, rather than the exception. Crime is common among teens: they are looking for excitement; they can't think of consequences. You now know, their 'judgements and control' wiring begins its development around 21 years of age."

Hero: *"Wow!* 🔔🔔🔔 *That explains heaps! Why don't I know this? It's so basic to our understanding of not just life, but to this stage of life!"*

Driver: "Hero is having another enlightened moment, Team! Give him a BIG cheer! We are *sooo* impressed with your progress Hero. 😊😊😊😊

We'll go into further detail on the Dunedin Study a little later, but to answer your question Hero: as I said earlier, most people don't see a connection between each stage. They generally go into denial at the mere mention of this kind of information, especially their relationship to their childhood. I can tell you from the number of people who *don't* sign up to our Courses after making an enquiry, that 'The survival system' is winning! Our course heroes are usually in a lot of pain with plenty of scar tissue by the time they enrol."

Teenager: "You can clearly see, when we give you our side of the rebellious teen image, that we are *not* rebelling!"

Hero: *"Speaking of rebelling: I remember the two biggest and most frustrating issues in my teens were that I wasn't taken seriously and no-one listened to me! My parents were still seeing me as a child. I sometimes had to stand up to them to be heard. Seeing this stage now from my parents' point of view, standing up would have looked like rebelling, wouldn't it?"*

Teenager: "I think most of us behave like that! We want a bit of empathy. We are going through a difficult transitioning time. A humorous way to look at it is: we don't create the problems; it's the nagging authority figures who are creating the problems in our lives when *they* don't understand the many complexities of this stage and what we are trying to achieve.

Teens struggle to make sense of this stage in their development too. It's like… what do you want from us? We're confused enough! Cut the pressure! We're feeling enough pressure from our peer group let alone all the other issues in this stage."

Driver interjecting: "Not only is the teen's intellectual brain insufficiently developed to think of consequences, he is undergoing changes to his physical self and he may also be trying to deal with other issues as well, such as:

- Hormones and their notorious imbalances

- Becoming a sexual being

- Trying to impress the opposite sex and his own sex

- Feeling pressure from parents, teachers and other authority figures

- Trying to decide on a course or a career path

- Feeling clumsy and awkward, even inept, in this new stage

- Comparing himself to the individuals in his peer group (not always favourably)

- *Seeking a sense of privacy*

- Trying to live with the conformity demands of his peer group

- Betrayal in love and sometimes those calling themselves a friend

- Seeking an outlet for emotional expression

- Social media pressures.

Can you think of any others Hero?"

Hero: *"Wow! Sure brings clarity to the pressures a lot of teens must be feeling!"*

Teenager: "Yep! Most of our course heroes are knocked out by the depth too. Can you handle more information Hero?"

Hero: *"Yes. Go ahead."*

Teenager: "When you were a teen Hero, trying to please so many people from different areas of your life, did one area exert more pressure than the others?"

Hero: *"I fitted in with my peer group okay, but it was my parents who exerted the most pressure, especially my dad."*

Teenager: "You were lucky you only felt pressure from one area. You could have also felt it from:

- Your extended family

- Your teachers and other authority figures

- Your peer group

- Yourself e.g., will I ever be enough? Will I fit in? Why do I feel different?

- More than one of these areas at the same time.

Hero: *"Like I said earlier, my pressure came from my parents. I remember the pressure I felt to follow in the family tradition and join the family business, you know... like father like son, like mother, like* daughter. I remember my father saying, "It's a tough world out there, very few succeed. I'm offering you security and status… a chance to make something of yourself. I don't want you to regret your decision in ten years' time." I did try. I swapped courses trying to fit in with my parents' wishes, but it wasn't for me.

I remember my parents, especially my dad, not being happy with my decision to go into advertising. I know I was a huge disappointment to them. It was a difficult time for everyone. He still reminds me that I missed a fabulous opportunity, but honestly, it would never have worked out for either of us.

Pulling the plug early was the right thing to do… even though I still feel uncomfortable, even a bit guilty about not living up to their expectations! As it turned out, my sister was the academic and fitted perfectly into that role. Old generational thinking of the eldest male always following in the family footsteps is still alive and well in my father's generation.

My younger brother left the family when he was 18, seeking an alternative lifestyle and bigger horizons. Last we heard; he was trekking in the Himalayas.

On the same subject: I have friends who wouldn't stand up to the family pressures. Later one of them was so depressed with his life and so fearful of breaking away from family tradition, he took his own life! We were all devasted! The others in my peer group who felt pressured into following in the family tradition live miserably, waiting for the hierarchy to pass away before making their move into freedom. The reasons are simple, aren't they? when you understand how 'The system' works."

Maturing Adult: "Yes. We've heard many similar stories from some of our other course heroes too. So sad and such a waste."

Driver: "I love listening to everyone involved in this conversation, but there's one thing that needs more clarity. It was mentioned earlier in the lead up to teen's story. Teens don't realise they are operating through their childhood model which has no self-responsibility – their carers were responsible for them. Suddenly their authority figures expect them to be responsible, but they've never learnt or been shown how to be responsible for themselves."

Hero: *"OMG! That makes so much sense to me!* 😕😕😕 *Even though I was accountable for my sister and brother, I did have trouble with the concept of self-responsibility. Not for long though… my parents were BIG on that stuff! That's where and when I started seriously thinking of self-responsibility as my personal power! Now I get it!!!"*

Driver: "Another breakthrough for our Hero, team. This is remarkable! We love working with you Hero! Congratulations! Three loud cheers for our Hero… hooray! 😊😊😊😊

Further, we know teens have no power or the financial resources to make life changing decisions for themselves at this stage, which adds further frustration and potential conflict with their authority figures."

Teenager: "Changing the subject, comparing yourself to others is never a good idea at any age, but we criticise ourselves harshly if we feel we are not living up to our peer groups' approval."

Driver interjecting: "The same as the child when he feels he's not living up to his carers' expectations."

Teenager: "Yep! We'll do almost anything to be accepted by our peer group. We present as strength in numbers, 'one rule fits all', follow the leader style, appearing formidable. 'Fear of rejection' from our generation keeps us tight! We need each other! **Presenting as a united front: it's us against the world!**"

Driver: "The system hasn't changed! It's 'The system' and its innate need to belong to the group for safety and survival that is the reason why teens want so badly to belong and to be accepted by their peer group!"

Hero: *"Got it! ♟♟♟ Total consistency, isn't it? All going back to our survival programming. It's true, we can't switch off these programs. They are borne into our DNA still helping us survive, even in the 21st Century. Remarkable!"*

Driver: "More awakening for Hero guys! We're so happy for you. Your life will never be the same. Onward and upward Hero! More cheers for our Hero team! Want to say hip, hip Child?" ☺☺☺☺

Teenager: "Hey Hero! Do you recall being pre-occupied with your appearance and how you behaved around your peers?"

Hero: *"I don't remember being preoccupied with my appearance so much as being aware that I had to conform with my peer group or risk rejection. I also remember there was an underlying sense of competition among us. Strange, I hadn't thought about that for years."*

Driver interjecting: "On the surface, it does seem like teenagers' rebel, doesn't it? But when we go deeper and really connect with what teens are being exposed to and what they are trying to achieve – even if they don't understand it themselves – I feel deep empathy for them.

Teen, did you have any knowledge of the issues you might be exposed to in this major transition?"

Teenager: "I had a general understanding of the challenges, but no specifics."

Driver: "You, Hero?"

Hero: *"No information, nothing! My parents didn't understand why I was standing up and reacting against their demands either. They still refer to teenagers as rebellious, as I did until now, rather than a major transition. It'll take a few more generations to change that perception, I'm guessing."*

Driver: "An important point: when we say teens want acceptance from their peer group, what we are really saying is they want *emotional acceptance* from their peer group. *Emotional acceptance* is how we feel good about ourselves, that we are accepted, we fit-in and we are okay. Emotional acceptance affirms our 'okayness'… new word! It goes hand in hand with emotional dependence on the group. All aligned with 'The group' and survival.

Hero, you can see how deeply and how emotionally dependent we are on our age group i.e. our generation. Hold that thought! We'll expand on this connection and its importance in the Maturing Adult time zone."

Teenager: "Okay. Changing the subject: do you remember anything that was a big deal for you in your teen years, Hero?"

Hero: *"Apart from not following in the family footsteps, not being heard or taken seriously, I remember privacy was a big deal for me."*

Teenager: "Lack of privacy *is* a big deal for teens. We are no longer children. Physically, in many ways… we are adults!"

Hero: *"Ah-ha! Of course.* 🔔🔔🔔 ***We are physically closer to an adult in size and hormonally than children. We do need privacy! Thanks teen!"***

Teenager to Driver: "Can I give cheers for Hero, this time?"

Driver: "Certainly can. You have given Hero a deep appreciation of your age and stage in life. Reap your reward Teenager."

Teenager: "Guys! Guess what! Another breakthrough for Hero and I did it for him this time! Give me a big cheer too! I've lost count of how many breakthroughs you've had Hero, but the Teenage breakthroughs are the best! Cheers for Hero and Teenager! ☺☺☺☺ You're okay Hero!"

Hero: *"Thanks Teen. You're okay too!"*

Driver: "Child, let's see your drawing and your colouring-in. Oh! Your drawing really does look like us. Look at Child's drawing everyone. Is that Hero! Oh! It looks like Hero, doesn't it? And your colouring-in is staying in the lines. That's so good. Would you like to pin your drawing on our Notice Board? I'll help you."

Child: "That will be fun. Do you have any red pins?"

Driver: "Yes, I do! Now let's hop back into the mighty Mustang and drive to the 'Maturing Adult' signpost. It's a fair distance from here so I'll turn on some easy listening music so everyone can relax for a while. How are you feeling Child? Are you a little sleepy? It's been a big day for you all of us, hasn't it?"

Child: "A bit. I'll have a cat nap."

Driver: "The music will help you drift off. We'll wake you when we're there. You can help Hero understand your part in his maturing age now. You are so important to us."

*The Dunedin Study, https://dunedinstudy.otago.ac.nz/studies

The Dunedin Multidisciplinary Health and Development Research Unit (The Dunedin Study) began in 1972 when the University of Otago Medical School, Dunedin, New Zealand, began following the lives of 1037 children born between 1st April, 1972 and 31st March, 1973. The study is ongoing and has the support of governments and industry throughout the world.

Hero's notes:

....

....

....

....

....

....

....

....

....

....

....

....

....

....

....

....

....

....

'MATURING ADULT' SIGNPOST

Driver: "We're nearly there. The 'Maturing Adult' signpost is coming into view. I'll pull in here. Great looking park. Let's alight and take in the fabulous view aka the overview of life.

Water, anyone? That bench and seating has the best view (pointing).

This is my favourite part of the Course when we gather all the stages together and make sense of the maturing adult's life.

Hero, the 'maturing adult' stage is *not* part of the survival system. We have outlived the programs designed for the first 35 years. This is the time zone when our thinking brain can transcend subconscious reactions and choose to intellectually respond to current circumstances.

I want to reinforce how the odds are stacked against 'The individual' ever reaching his potential. We're going to change that! Conformity is the number one issue today in *all* time zones. Conforming with the tribe when we lived in a cave with only 'The Pack' to protect us, meant survival.

But, what about now? Who says we must conform and hand over our personal power and free will to a non-intellectual survival system that is dumbing us down and stunting 'The individual' and our potential today. Where does that rule come from?

The 'ganging up' effect of conforming, to use Hero's fabulous term, is felt even more in midlife and beyond:

- The rules and conditioning from your childhood are still coming through subconsciously.

- So too your subconscious reactions from your childhood model beliefs and copied generational behaviours.

- Fear will always remind you of the possibility of rejection.

- The 'Pack' mentality of your peer group/generation expects you to conform.

- The status quo and its 'crowd mentality' is doubling down on the adult to conform.

Now I've set the scene 'Maturing Adult', are you ready to help Hero understand your time zone and why independent adult behaviour is labelled a 'Midlife Crisis' and why it's not?"

Maturing Adult: "Always ready Boss."

Teenager sniggering: "What a suck!"

Maturing Adult ignoring Teen's comment: "Most of us live unconsciously obeying the rules and conditioning we learnt in the first half of our lives, wondering why, in the maturing stage of life, we feel 'stuck' and powerless. There are no rules in midlife! It's 'The system' repeating itself with its subconscious *reactive* way of surviving.

I love to watch our Heroes' reactions when I casually say, 'The Midlife Crisis is not a crisis'. The so-called Midlife Crisis has been misinterpreted. It's the maturing adult transitioning into independence from 'The group', whoever they are, and the group's conformity expectations.

It's the maturing adult saying 'no' to conformity! 'no' to all the rules! and 'no' to our conditioning from childhood and our teen years. He is choosing to reset old programs using his personal

power and free will and to make choices that work in his best interests today that are being mistaken for or misinterpreted as delinquent adult behaviour."

Driver interrupting: "A case in point: I recently read where a man in his mid-forties bought himself a Porsche and was immediately labelled as having a Midlife Crisis. He said it had taken him that long, with all his other financial commitments, to save for the car of his dreams; he never considered the purchase to be a midlife crisis response.

Without knowledge of our survival programming and without an overview of life, it's easy for us and some professionals too, to think that a maturing adult who is showing signs of independence from generational and status quo conformity, must be having a 'Midlife Crisis'."

Maturing Adult: "What's really happening is: we've outlived the reactive, kneejerk survival system. We've outgrown our conditioning and all its rules; conforming and fitting in as we did in the first half of our lives. We realise we are all different and it's okay to be different. We now have an evolving intellectual brain. Let's use it!

Midlife is about transitioning from our conditioning and transcending the rules... if we are brave enough, choosing to live by our own Code of conduct."

Teenager excitedly butting in: "Yeah! Like I'm transitioning from my childhood and forming a new alliance with my generation."

Driver: "Excellent comparison Teen!

Teenager made the comparison that his age group is transitioning from childhood and forming a new alliance with his generation;

**The maturing adult is transitioning from the first
half of his life and forming a new alliance
with himself and his independence.**

Basically, when we want approval from an individual or a group, above self-approval, we are giving 'them' our power."

Hero: *"Let me paraphrase. In midlife, my feelings of powerlessness are coming from being 'stuck' in subconscious reactive beliefs and behaviours learnt in the first half of my life. 'Stuck' like a broken record when I have no understanding of survival forces or deny their existence. Is that right?"*

Maturing Adult: "Yes. All the above reasons are now making your maturing adult time zone *feel* powerless and ineffective. So yes, to use another of your fab expressions, we become 'stuck' like a broken record."

Driver interjecting: "Remember, we didn't live longer than 35 years when the programs were built into our DNA. Today, 35 years is only the first half of our lives!"

Maturing Adult: "Midlife has no rules. Timewise, midlife is *not* part of the survival system! We are free agents today... this is our time now. A time to stretch our wings and decide for ourselves if we want to bring our potential to life or live as we were conditioned to live in childhood and teen years and stay huddled in 'The group' and its conforming mentality.

Powerful choices await the conscious mind!"

Hero: *"OMG! It's as simple as it is complicated, isn't it?"*

Maturing Adult: "Sure is. The good news: this is your opportunity to rewrite the programs running in your head to suit your maturing self today – taking responsibility for yourself, making way for 'The individual' and its place in history. No longer robotically working with life and empowering 'The group', but rather, seeking your own approval above 'group' approval and deciding how life will work for you in the second half of your life… *if you have the courage.*"

Driver: "Maturing Adult and I have lots more to help you in this time zone, Hero, including the silent power of your emotional life.

You'll soon make even more sense of Aristotle's quote: *"Give me a child until he is seven and I will show you the man."*

Hero, do you remember in the Childhood time zone, you asked for examples of the time zone differences between your inner child and maturing adult? I asked if you would wait until we added the Teenage stage."

Hero: *"I do remember. I'm curious to learn how the time zones fully relate to each other at my age."*

Driver: "There are dozens of subjects in the Childhood Model with child/adult time zone differences, such as:

- The 'Need to belong' – an innate force

- Choices

- Conformity

- Time and change

- The 'personal' serious world of a child

- Fear

- Perfection

- All you need is love

- Emotional dependence.

Hero, would you like to choose three that could be impacting your life today?"

Hero: *"Mmm... The need to belong – an innate force, sounds interesting. How about choices and conformity. Oh, and learning more about fear would be good too."*

Child: "That's four. I can count!" ☺

Driver: "Hello Child. Yes! You're right. You deserve another star ★ You are so clever and bright as a little button after your cat nap. Hero *did* choose four!"

Child: "I love my stars. I have three now."

Driver: "Yes you do! Hero, you need to understand:

You can never cut/sever the cords to your hardwired subconscious survival kneejerk reactions, but you can disarm their 'live' power with new awareness and a considered intellectual response... to build a 'dream-team' Higher consciousness with your inner child."

Maturing Adult: "These examples will instantly clarify another layer of why you've been feeling 'stuck' and powerless and why 'The Midlife Crisis' has been seen as delinquent adult behaviour, rather than satisfying your maturing needs and duty to yourself. We'll start with:

YOUR 'NEED TO BELONG' – AN INNATE FORCE:

As you now know, belonging to 'The Pack' was the caveman's way of surviving. Today, our innate 'Need to belong' and dependence on 'The group' for emotional support in the first half of our lives becomes an unconscious, intimidating force, often conflicting with our maturing needs.

Childhood years: Briefly, our very survival depends on someone caring for us, doesn't it? Our primal Will to survive translates into a 'Need to belong' to be cared for and protected. Abandonment is a primal fear.

Teenage years: Teens shift alliances from the tribal family to their generation. Not fitting in, exclusion and fear of rejection from their peer group is dangerous territory for teens. That's how important a sense of belonging and its emotional support is, in the first half of our lives!

The unaware *reactive* adult is 'stuck', feeling powerless and frustrated. He wants a bigger life, but he doesn't understand that fear, his innate 'need to belong' and dependence on others for emotional support keeps him in a holding position. Feelings of 'stuckness' is one of the first signs his emotional life is ready to expand and support him.

The aware maturing adult acknowledges his yearning for independence. He understands the two time zones and realises he no longer 'needs to belong' for childhood survival or for his teenage generation's acceptance and emotional support. Emotional dependence on others interferes with his maturing position and belongs to the past. He is now a separate and complete entity, free to make independent choices to progress his life... *if he has the courage."*

Driver interjecting: "It's a courageous move to review and upgrade everything you were conditioned to believe in the first half of your life. This is part of the pain of letting go of childhood and teenage beliefs. To risk rejection by your generation and/or the status quo at 40 years old or older is more intimidating to most people than forging an independent path. That's why so few people are willing to do it! I'll give you an example of this later. Needing to belong and fearing rejection keeps most of us 'living small', huddled in 'the group's approval', and not fulfilling our obligations to 'the self' and its potential."

Hero: *"Ah-ha!* 🔔🔔🔔 *That makes perfect sense. I know sometimes I knuckle under, fearing rejection if I make an independent decision that's not aligned with the group and its current thinking, especially in business. You're right! Such clarity!"*

Driver: "Another breakthrough for Hero team! Fearing rejection if he makes an independent decision! **This is the kind of clarity that changes lives.** Give Hero a big applause. (Everyone clapping and cheering) ☺☺☺☺

Maturing Adult, to help Hero understand more deeply the innate power of belonging, would you like to expand on the 'Need to belong' and the status quo today."

Maturing Adult: "Sure Boss. Makes sense. Listen up Hero.

YOUR 'NEED TO BELONG' AND THE STATUS QUO TODAY:

Let's find out how your childhood and teenage 'Need to belong' work against the maturing individual's desire for independence today.

The unaware *reactive* adult has little understanding of his innate 'Need to belong'. Fear of rejection, fear of self-expression, criticism or judgement from 'The group' and its conforming mentality, keep him contained in his fear-based comfort zones, emotionally stunted and not living up to his potential for fear of upsetting family, friends, neighbours and relationships' wider social circles.

The aware maturing adult rationalises that he no longer 'needs to belong' for survival or acceptance, neither does he have to conform with the group and its rules. It's time for him to live on his own terms and to make independent choices to satisfy his maturing needs. He is seeking his own approval, not just above his generation's approval, but above status quo approval per se! Huge!

I have a question for you Hero: Is fear of rejection adding to your feelings of powerlessness? In other words, does a need for acceptance by your peers make you unwilling to risk rejection? Is there anything you are *not* doing for fear of upsetting the people around you?"

Hero: *"Wow! ☺☺☺ I've never associated my fear of rejection with feelings of powerlessness. Of course, they must be connected. I need to decide whether I'm willing to risk rejection and live independently or live safe within the fold, never realising my potential. This is huge, isn't it?"*

Driver: "More bells ringing for Hero, team. Now Hero is associating his fear of rejection with not only making an independent decision, but also with his deeper feelings of powerlessness. Love this! You are our Hero, Hero! Let's hear it for Hero guys. Hooray!" ☺☺☺☺

Maturing Adult: "Now let's delve into Choices and see if that helps you further. Child, are you ready to help Hero understand Choices?"

CHOICES:

Child: "Yes. As a literal child, I don't understand what choices mean. I live in a 'now' world that is black-or-white, yes-or-no, right-or-wrong, can-or-can't, should-or-shouldn't."

Maturing Adult: "**The unaware *reactive* adult** feels frustrated and 'stuck' in a world that superficially appears to have no alternative choices and no wriggle room. A black-or-white mindset may also indicate, especially in business, that this adult has not evolved in his personal development. Trying to work with an inflexible, reactive, either/or mindset is difficult for everyone, not just for the unaware adult.

The aware maturing adult rationalises that his life can be summed up by the choices he makes or the choices someone else makes for him. Choices are at the heart of his freedom. Grey areas of negotiation and conciliation and alternative choices give him lots of wriggle room and incredible power to express himself and to expand his emotional freedom exponentially. There is no going back to the suffocating either/or world of his 'backseat driver'. No offence Child."

Child: "I don't know what you mean."

Maturing Adult: "Just grown-up stuff Child. You did a great job. Here's another question for you Hero: were you taught as a child that choices made in your best interests were selfish?"

Hero: *"Wow! 🔔🔔🔔 Yes. It was a childhood rule, just like I had to share everything. I'll upgrade both those learnt behaviours to fit in with current time. Thanks for that realisation."*

Driver: "More bells ringing for Hero guys! Love this! Well done Hero! This Course really explains the two-time zone system, doesn't it?" ☺☺☺☺

Maturing Adult: "Excellent work Hero! Let's see if we can prompt another breakthrough for you when we check out Conformity. We feel safe in the fold, don't we? Ready to help Hero with Conformity, Child? Teen, you're on soon."

CONFORMITY:

Child: "I was programmed to conform like all the other kids. I don't understand what conformity means. I just 'follow the leader'. I learnt there was safety in numbers and fitting in was a good thing and that one rule suited all of us, but secretly, sometimes I feel I don't fit in all the time."

Teenager: "You know that teenagers are swapping alliances from the tribal family to their peer group for emotional acceptance. That means that if we want to belong to our peer group/our generation, we *must* conform or risk rejection. It's either or. There's no other way."

Maturing Adult: "The unaware *reactive* adult doesn't under that fear, childhood beliefs, dependence on peer group support and its 'Pack' mentality are all contributing to his feelings of 'stuckness' and powerlessness and to his frustration. He even squashes his maturing needs and his potential for fear of upsetting family, friends and wider social circles. Conforming sucks the power from this individual.

The aware maturing adult now conscious of the two time zones, is also awake to tribal and generational conditioning and conformity expectations. This empowered adult also acknowledges and respects his emotional maturing needs. He reasons, he is not rebelling against his generation or the status quo, but rather, he is choosing to make independent decisions that work in his best interests today – the awakened adult's rite of passage.

I have another question for you Hero: How big could your life be without conformity issues? With a little bit of courage, what's the first thing you could do to own your power? Tiny steps."

Hero: *"The first thing I could do is to say 'No' occasionally, especially when I'm feeling under the hammer. Usually, I try to be obliging even when I know I'm adding more pressure to myself. I like your questions. They make me think!"*

Maturing Adult: "Good to know Hero. Ready to learn more about Fear?"

Hero: *Nodding.*

FEAR:

Maturing Adult: "Fear was/is part of our survival DNA. Fear warned us of imminent physical danger when we lived in a hostile environment with a much shorter lifespan. Our adrenals reacted to fear with 'fight or flight' reactions making us stronger and faster, helping us escape physical danger. Nothing has changed! Fear's job has always been to keep us safe; it's still an extremely good warning system. **I like to think of fear as my personal bodyguard.**

Now let's put it all together. Child… you're on!"

Child: "Okay. Fear makes me scared and keeps me in my comfort zones. I instinctively obey fear or I might get into trouble. My intellectual brain is still in its simple stages of development. I don't understand the difference between a real fear and a perceived fear. Every time fear is present, I retreat."

Maturing Adult: "**The unaware *reactive* adult** is unlikely to go against his fear-based childhood comfort zones. He continues to be managed and limited by fear and its intimidatory survival tactics. This adult doesn't understand where his fear is coming from. His emotional life remains on hold as he continues to live frustratingly under his potential. Without an intellectual understanding of fear and its role in our survival, anxiousness and 'settling' may become a way of life for this individual.

The aware maturing adult realises that most of his fears are his inner child's fears i.e., perceived fears from his childhood. He also realises that when he expands his childhood comfort zones, or when he moves into unknown territory, he will automatically feel anxious and fearful. Understanding this, the aware adult can progress, with fear accompanying him, as it should… no longer determining the size of his life."

Hero: *"Wow! 🔔🔔🔔 Now I 'get' why I feel anxious when I'm out there, or in unfamiliar territory, or standing up and saying what I need or simply asking for assistance. Not sure where that comes from… probably childhood too."*

Maturing Adult: "You are really getting this stuff, aren't you? Let's hear it for Hero, guys! I've lost count of how many breakthroughs. Now he understands where his anxiety is coming from. Major stuff! Three cheers for our Hero! Hooray! ☺☺☺☺

One more thing: Apart from adrenaline junkies ☺ most of us like to feel safe and secure, not just in childhood but throughout our lives, which is another reason why fear is sooo intimidating."

Driver interjecting: "Did you know, fear loves surprises? It's in its element when you are surprised by an unexpected outcome. Then it can really ramp up your anxiety!"

Hero: *"This is making so much sense to me. When something catches me off-guard, I immediately feel my adrenaline kicking in and reacting to my current situation."*

Maturing Adult: "You're like a duck to water, Hero. Well done!

Now let's give you more empowering information for use in 'real-time' Hero."

Hero's notes:

SECTION III:

LIVING IN 'REAL-TIME'

THE THREE MAJOR POWER BASES IN OUR LIVES

Driver: "The best way to understand our major power bases Hero, including emotional independence, is to go back to our childhood and work our way forward:

- First, we were born with our *feelings*, senses, instincts and fear all helping us to survive.

- **Our feeling/emotional life was demoted in order of importance when our intellectual brain took over around the age of seven years old and has remained on hold since then.**

- By the age of 21, we are physically fully developed.

- Our intellectual brain continues restructuring and rewiring itself until around 25 years.

- **Now in the maturing adult time zone,** our emotional right-side brain wants to catch up to *her* fully developed physical and intellectual counterparts to expand our choices and move us forward into the adult rite of passage... *if we have the courage.*

I say, '*if we have the courage*' a lot, don't I? ☺

> **Your emotional life is the backbone of your life.**
>
> **She, your right-side brain, is your courage.**
>
> **He, your left-side brain, is your reasoning.**

How are you going with this, Hero?"

Hero: *"Of course. We talk about being ballsy or having the guts or the courage to do something, don't we? What we really mean is our emotional life has come of age and she now wants to help expand our boundaries. Right?"*

Driver: "Yes! And, Hero, just to be clear, emotional expansion, emotional expression and emotional independence are our acts of courage. You've never learnt the value of your emotional life, have you?

Now it's 'her' turn to mature and complete the cycles of our development i.e., physical, intellectual and emotional. She gives you an opportunity to broaden your emotional life to meet your maturing needs. She is saying 'move over'… make room for me. It's my time now! She's the one that decides how big your life can be… *if you have the courage!* ☺ There, I've said it again!"

Hero: ***"Oh wow!*** 🔔🔔🔔 ***I never realised how our physical, intellectual and emotional development have such a logical developmental sequence. Surely not a random thing… The Universe has certainly thought this through to perfection. It's amazing, isn't it! Emotional independence is our courage in midlife and another reason why the midlife crisis has been misinterpreted. Excellent insights!"***

Driver: "Team! More bells ringing for Hero. He 'gets' the three power bases and their progressive development over our lives. And Hero now understands emotional independence is emotional courage. Give him a loud cheer! Well done Hero! Excellent! ☺☺☺☺

Child and Teenager, please give Hero your understanding of emotional dependence and then Maturing Adult can bring Hero up to speed on emotional *independence*. This is such an important part of our lives, but I doubt it is fully understood. Ready guys? Child, you're on."

Hero's notes:

....

....

....

....

....

....

....

....

....

....

....

....

....

....

....

....

....

....

DISTINCTIONS BETWEEN EMOTIONAL DEPENDENCE AND EMOTIONAL *IN*DEPENDENCE:

Child: "I need a family or someone to care for me or I won't survive. That means I rely on those people to love and protect me, not only to keep me physically safe, but also, I need their support on an emotional level, so I feel okay about myself. Feeling supported and safe are probably the two most important things at my age, otherwise it's a very scary place."

Teenager: "Hero! As you know, teenagers shift alliances from their tribal family to their generation. It's a big and important shift. It's not only acceptance we want from our peer group, but we also want their emotional support to feel okay about ourselves; that we've 'made it' with our generation. Exclusion or rejection makes the alienated teen feel he doesn't belong anywhere! It's dangerous territory for teens. That's how important a sense of belonging and its emotional support really is, in the teenage time zone."

Maturing Adult: "The unaware *reactive* adult has not reconciled that his 'Need to belong' and dependence on others for acceptance and emotional support keeps him fitting in and conforming, adding to his current feelings of powerlessness and frustration. He finds it difficult to stand up and say what he wants or needs and he doesn't understand why he feels 'stuck', caught between his emotional dependence on others for support to feel okay about himself and his maturing desire for some independence.

The aware maturing adult recognises and acknowledges his need for independence. He understands 'The system' and its two time zones and he is willing to transcend old beliefs that are not working for him today e.g. selfishness and sharing. He adjusts his childhood coping behaviours to fit his maturing stage of life and reviews and updates his self-image. He is no longer reliant on others for emotional support to feel okay about himself. He can lean on himself and endorse his own approval. Acknowledgement that he is now a single, separate and complete entity with no strings to the outside world, allows him to make emotionally independent choices to progress his life… *if he has the courage.*

Hey Hero! How will this new understanding of emotional independence from others, impact your life?"

Hero: *"Let me count the ways. Wow!* 😊😊😊 *Emotional independence is what it's all about at my age, isn't it? … leaning on and supporting myself, taking responsibility for all the decisions I make, with or without 'the group' or anyone's approval. Emotional dependence and emotional independence is a bit like separating the men from the boys, isn't it? Emotional independence is our power base in my time zone. As you say… if we have the courage."*

Maturing Adult: "Everyone! Hero just had another enlightened moment… emotional dependence and emotional independence is like separating the men from the boys! Great comparison Hero! We are sooo impressed! Let's hear it for Hero! Hooray!" ☺☺☺☺

Hero: *"I just realised something else. Emotional dependence on others at my age to feel okay about myself, gives 'them' all my power, doesn't it? Of course. I didn't understand that!* 😊😊😊 *More clarity as to where my feelings of 'stuckness' and powerlessness have been coming from."*

Maturing Adult: "Guys! You're not going to believe this! This is a two-in-one conscious moment! A first for us! Hero just realised emotional dependence on others for support *at his age*, gives them all his power. Cheers Hero! Congratulations. We love how you've picked up the nuances of emotional independence! Loud cheers for Hero!" ☺☺☺☺

Driver: "Ready for more reveals Hero?

Hero's notes:

....
....
....
....
....
....
....
....
....
....
....
....
....
....
....
....
....

THE POWER OF YOUR EMOTIONAL LIFE

"When you dismiss the power and the value of your emotional life, you become disconnected from your inner life. If you haven't included your feelings in your decision-making, *how do you know if the decision is the right one for you?* I know my 'intellectual only' decisions eventually became increasingly difficult and frustrating to live with. My life felt empty and stressed, rather than filled with passion, joy and purpose.

Hero, I believe this is another reason why so many people change careers and lifestyles in midlife. They're done with the 'intellectual only' life and are going after a more emotionally satisfying life. They are incorporating and trusting their feelings in their decision-making, to resonate with and confirm their new direction.

When we don't include our feelings, we feel out of balance and disconnected from our inner life. It's also the reason why we seek comfort in drugs, alcohol and/or food, to name a few.

With only our over-functioning intellect making the decisions, we go straight to the pantry, fridge etc. trying to satisfy the feelings we haven't acknowledged!"

Hero: *"Got it! Our emotional life is totally undervalued, isn't it? It's a major power base since birth but the intellect has been given superiority, especially in recent history. Is it possible to harmonise our three power bases?"*

Driver: "Yes. Try giving each a say in your day-to-day transactions with yourself."

Hero: *"OMG!* 🔔🔔🔔 *My three power bases would love that, especially my physical self that reminds me when I don't make*

the time, how much better I feel with exercise. Our inner life is like your Mustang's V8 power, isn't it? All hidden away and out of sight."

Driver: "Team. Another breakthrough for Hero! He just compared his inner life to the Mighty Mustang's V8 power being under the bonnet. Fabulous break-through Hero! Amazing! Love this! ☺☺☺☺

Now let's help Hero make sense of his child/adult self-image.

Hero's notes:

. . . .

. . . .

. . . .

. . . .

. . . .

. . . .

. . . .

. . . .

. . . .

. . . .

. . . .

. . . .

. . . .

. . . .

. . . .

. . . .

. . . .

MAKING SENSE OF YOUR CHILD/ADULT SELF-IMAGE

Driver: Okay team, ready for the spotlight again? Child, you're up first. Give Hero an understanding of how you built your self-image, then Teen… you know the drill."

Child: "My beliefs about me are literal. My sense of self i.e., my self-esteem and self-worth… everything to do with my identity were formed from the feedback I received and interpreted from my carers and other external sources. I confirmed the feedback on an instinctual and feeling level by how people reacted to me and the tone in their words. I accept their comments literally at face value because my intellectual brain is not developed enough to question, reason or discriminate. I take all their comments to heart. Remember how I feel when people call me stupid? I feel the same way when people's comments are not nice."

Teenager: "Honestly, some people must think I have no feelings! When they call me names and judge me harshly, a few remarks really stick. Those remarks and comments impact who I think I can be, especially if they are said by people who are close to me. I feel the same as Child when I hear unconstructive criticism or insensitive comments."

Maturing Adult: "The unaware *reactive* adult continues to live from the opinions of others from an earlier time zone to validate his feelings about himself and his identity today. This creates more self-doubt and adds more fuel to not liking himself. Remaining in the little kid's image (no offence Child) or trying to live with hurtful comments or defining moments from his teens, the unaware adult feels 'less than', or 'not enough', his self-doubts impacting his drive to go after what he wants or feeling that he is not capable of being more.

The aware maturing adult with his new understanding is working with his updated, empowered self-image, acknowledging his many talents, qualifications, life education, experiences and wisdom today. He is no longer stunted by outdated, 'were they ever real' beliefs or comments. He admits he's okay, that he is a work-in-progress, inspired and loving it."

Hero: *"You make it all sound so logical!"*

Maturing Adult: "Thank you; it really is logical when you understand survival forces. Hero, do you remember any words or phrases from childhood that hurt you or any defining moments? Has any childhood image or any feelings or beliefs from childhood or your teenage years held you back?"

Hero: *"I do remember a couple of hurtful words from childhood and a few harsh remarks made about me in my teens, especially when I decided not to follow in my family footsteps. Do you really think they are impacting me to that extent today?"*

Maturing Adult: "Count on it! *'Sticks and stones will break my bones, but names will never hurt me.'* Not true – words can be toxic. Harsh words, emotionally intense comments or defining moments from the first half of our lives that haven't been acknowledged, continue to haunt the unaware adult, all adding to his self-doubts and disliking himself today.

Add to this, all the controls, standards, conformity expectations, dependence issues etc. from childhood and teen years... it's enough weight to stop most adults moving forward, especially without knowledge of our survival system and the programs running in our heads.

To help you move forward Hero, the first and most basic thing you can do is to start liking yourself."

Hero's notes:

....
....
....
....
....
....
....
....
....
....
....
....
....
....
....
....
....
....

LIKING YOURSELF: YOUR CATALYST FOR CHANGE

Driver: "Most of us don't think too much about the crossover between child, teenage and adult time zones. Our age and time simply move us forward. Liking yourself is a huge breakthrough.

Hero: *"I've never thought about the differences between liking or not liking myself. How will liking myself be the catalyst for change?"*

Driver: "Great question, Hero. The relationship you have with yourself sets the tone for all areas of your life. Basically, liking yourself will change your attitude towards yourself. Self-love, self-approval and an updated self-image will unite with your Higher conscious needs and allow life-changing possibilities, such as:

- Becoming more courageous.

- No longer allowing others to be more important than you.

- A new sense of inner security with no strings to the outside world.

- You'll be more likely to speak up on matters important to you.

- Less intimidated by fear, change, those in authority or stronger personalities.

- Allowing emotionally independent choices to expand and build a more satisfying life."

Hero: *"You mention personal power a lot. What exactly do you mean?"*

Driver: "Glad you asked. Personal power is independent and free thinking associated with free will, choices and the right to be yourself. It's the consummate act of choosing to live by your Code of behaviour – an empowered adult, congruent with his stage of life, *liberating emotional dependence and conformity issues from his childhood and teenage 'belonging' years.* Personal power lives quietly and peacefully within the adult who has ventured back to 'the self' and has given himself permission and the authority to take full responsibility for himself, *with or without others' approval.*"

Hero: *"Wow!* 😟😟😟 *Now I understand why most people never get to own their personal power and use their free will. Just like you said earlier, the odds are stacked against 'The individual' ever reaching his potential and his independence. Conformity and compliance are the issues in all time zones, aren't they? Our programmed 'Need to belong' to the group is powerfully intimidating, isn't it?"*

Driver: "Another win for Hero guys! Great work Hero! Cheers! ☺☺☺☺

While Child and Teen are off kicking the football, would you like to hear a story about our unconscious "Need to belong?"

Hero: *"Sounds good."*

Maturing Adult: "I like stories too."

Driver: "Before I became aware of our programmed lives and long before I started these Courses, I ran a Classic Glamour Services business. At the time, my research hadn't connected our programmed lives with my clients' 'fear of rejection' reactions.

The Classic Glamour Services three-hour session was designed for each client and included anatomic makeup techniques, hairstyling to suit the client's face shape and colours complimentary to hair and skin tones from seasonal colour swatches.

Looking at their enhanced image at the end of the step-by-step course, draped in one of their complimentary colours, with makeup and hairstyling to suit their face shape, 90% of my clients would say, *'I can't look like this!'* They would mention their husbands liked them to 'look natural', or their friends and family wouldn't understand, or they might think she wanted to be better than them.

My clients were choosing, without knowledge of our programmed survival forces, to live beneath their enhanced image for fear of upsetting someone important in their lives, perhaps fearing rejection or not feeling they were worthy or deserving of looking so beautiful.

Fear of offending a VIP and/or fear of rejection are often more intimidating than making independent choices."

Hero: *"Our 'Need to belong' sure has a hold over us when we don't understand basic survival programs, doesn't it?"*

Maturing Adult: "More reinforcement of group power."

Driver: "Yes. Belonging and conforming to the group and its rules are undeniable unconscious survival forces.

Ah, excellent timing Child and Teenager. You're back from playing footy. Okay team, look around you. Have we picked up behind us? Great. Back into 'The Legend' and let's drive to the office.

Child, as soon as we get back, let's find those red pins and hang your drawing on our Notice Board. And then, would you like to give Hero a copy of the four Handouts. They are all numbered. We know you can count. Can you recognise numbers too? We are all so proud of you!

Fabulous teamwork, guys! You've excelled. What a memorable day this has been for all of us!"

Hero's notes:

....

....

....

....

....

....

....

....

....

....

....

....

....

....

....

....

....

....

SECTION IV: HOMEWORK

REINVENTING YOURSELF & MEETING YOUR POTENTIAL

BUILDING AN UPDATED HIGH-OCTANE SELF-IMAGE

Driver: "We're back safe and sound. Thanks to the mighty Mustang! Would you like to freshen up and I'll put the jug on. Coffee, tea anyone? There's plenty of milk, water and cool drinks in the fridge. Sugar and a choice of biscuits are in the marked containers on the bench.

Teen, please look after Child. Make sure he has a cool drink and something to eat. Everyone, please make your way to the office/classroom by quarter past. Okay?

***

To make it easy, let's run through how we've set up your Homework, Hero. Any questions over the next few weeks, please phone or email me.

I see you've handed Hero the four Handouts Child. Well done and thank you.

Hero, I have a fifth Handout re your feelings of 'stuckness' and powerlessness. This extra Handout has more to do with what may be happening currently in your personal life rather than a connection to survival programming. We like to think we've covered all the bases for our Heroes." ☺

Hero: *"Thank you. Most unexpected."*

Driver: "I'd like to start this Section by saying most of us learnt to be hard on ourselves as children and teens. Harsh then; harsh now. 'Not enough' then; 'not enough' now. The maturing part of our lives gives us an opportunity to cut ourselves some slack and dismiss the monkey mind always chipping away at our

85

self-esteem. We need to be kinder and gentler on ourselves, treating ourselves as we would a kitten or a child. Handout 3: Self-talk and affirmations will help you encourage and promote yourself and your personal power Hero.

Unlike your childhood and teen years, where 'different' was a stigma and at odds with conformity, in this stage, we're done with the traditional conforming mindset and its straitjacket effects, living in mediocrity and the sameness philosophy. It's your time now:

- 'Different' is good.

- 'Different' is satisfying.

- 'Different' is unique and powerful.

As you know, your emotional independence from 'The group' is a major power base in your maturing life. You are admitting to yourself that with all your different life experiences, life education, qualifications, wisdom etc., you *are* different and at last, it's okay to be 'different' and to break away from sameness and mediocrity. 'The individual' and his differences are an awesome power base today.

Conforming with the tribe made perfect sense in caveman times. But now with our intellectual brain able to think for itself, how can we all be the same? How can we all think the same way or be the same at 40, 50, 60 years old or older?

- Taking ownership of your life is powerful.

- No longer the first half of your life dictating how you are supposed to think, behave and live for the rest of your life.

- Giving yourself permission to reinvent yourself and to meet your potential is your maturing 'rite of passage'.

- Emotional independence is your new power base.

**Emotional independence can be seen as
the misinterpreted Midlife Crisis.**

Now, it's about the importance of your inner world and the changes that appear in your exterior world when you like yourself, working with an inspiring, up-to-date self-image, building confidence and new beliefs in yourself and making choices that work in your best interests, congruent with who you are today in the maturing adult time zone.

Hero, you've been very quiet. How are you going with all this?"

Hero: *"I'm just taking it all in. I've said it before, 'The Mastering Course' makes everything seem so logical and so clear."*

Driver: "Thank you Hero, on behalf of 'The Team'.

Now we're focusing on your Homework Hero. Let's help you build an empowering self-image. First, become aware of your internal dialogue i.e., the words and phrases you use regularly when speaking to yourself. Are they uplifting and encouraging, do they build your confidence, or do they diminish your adult self-image? Are any/most from your childhood and teen years?

Remember Hero: you are disarming automatic subconscious reactions i.e., old programs running in your head: harsh old programs that diminish you today.

To help you *feel the difference* between the two time zones, and to help you align your new self-image with current time, upgrade your choice of words and phrases… really resonate with the words you choose to be part of your updated self-image. Make them special words that mean something to you. Maybe choose some words and phrases you can grow into, that make it even more challenging and highly motivational. Handout 3 will help get you started.

This is about creating an 'upbeat rave review' about you and your updated qualifications, life education, experiences, achievements, including issues you've overcome, how proud you felt of yourself. Who do you want to be? What would this *feel* like/look like to you? Create a powerful self-image that will transcend your inner child's destiny and your baggage. Be Bold!

You are a work in progress. Continue to update your image from time to time. An up-to-date self-image will invite all kinds of wonderful things into your life and the courage to go after them… even if you feel like an impostor the first time, second time, every time! Action brings your power to life and acting the part will build your confidence and a new belief in yourself."

Hero: *"I'm going to have lots of fun setting up my new self-image. Can't wait to supersede all the old limiting beliefs I've been trying to live with since who knows when. And all the stuff I've put in my own way. Thanks guys!"*

Driver: "The Team and I have high hopes for you Hero. You have excelled at every turn. We will always be here cheering you on! Don't forget that! Now let's expand your new self-image with Your Courage Shopping List."

Hero's updated high-octane self-image:

....

....

....

....

....

....

....

....

....

....

....

....

....

....

....

....

....

YOUR COURAGE SHOPPING LIST

Driver: "Your courage shopping list is about working with and *feeling your passion*. We're done with the 'intellectual only' life and now you're expanding your emotional life, pursuing emotional expression, emotional satisfaction and emotional independence.

This is a grand opportunity to own up and embrace everything you've been silencing or *not* daring to consider, taking your dreams from improbable to possible and then to actual!

Hey Hero, before we shake up your courage, have you given any more thought to Maturing Adult's question earlier: How big could your life be without conformity issues? Any more thoughts?"

Hero: *"Not conformity so much, but I just realised, challenges in this stage usually relate to expanding a fear-based boundary or expanding my emotional life and making independent choices. It takes a lot of courage, doesn't it?"*

Maturing Adult and Driver in unison: "Yes… that's why so few people do it!"

Hero: *"I'm beginning to admire people whose independent behaviour is labelled a Midlife Crisis. 😄😄😄 I hope someone labels me!"* ☺

Driver: "Team, listen to this! Remember when Hero said at the beginning of this course, he would be totally humiliated being called out as having a midlife crisis? Hero now hopes someone *does* call him out as having a Midlife Crisis! You've come such a long way Hero! No stopping you now. Cheers from The Team. Hooray! ☺☺☺☺

Hero, now you understand your emotional life in this stage is your courage and key to satisfying your maturing adult needs, stretch your imagination... if there was no conformity and no emotional dependent issues:

- What would you love to do?

- What would you buy?

- Would you relocate?

- Would you go after a more emotionally satisfying career?

- Would you change your lifestyle?

- Would you start a business?

- Would you ask someone special out on a date?

- Would you go after a promotion?

- Would you take that trip you've been shelving for years?

- Which affirmations from Handout 3 will encourage you?

Leave your courage shopping list in plain sight for the next week or so and allow your thoughts and ideas to flow through freely. Nothing is ruled out... forget fear and your old comfort zones, override all the things you were told you can't do or you can't have. Include everything, even things you consider imaginary or unobtainable right now!

Project manage your life. See your life as something you are building. Visualise what you want, then plan a series of small steps back to where you are now. Handout 2: How to work with your subconscious mind today will help bring your courage shopping list to life.

You may also like to set up a Vision Board where you attach pictures, photos, quotations etc. anything that inspires you. Keep updating your Vision Board to maintain your inspiration.

Incorporating short and long-term visions into your courage shopping list will help you stay focused. e.g., where you'd like to be in say a year's time, two years' time? Five, ten years from now."

Hero: *"What a challenging and motivational way to end what has been a fabulous journey through time. I can't wait to see the changes I make to my life thanks to your 'Mastering Course'. I'll write a five-star review and recommend it to everyone. Thank you."*

Driver: "It's been a privilege Hero. Please stay in touch and let's know when you've been called out as having a Midlife Crisis! Best wishes and much success from the Team!" ☺☺☺☺

Hero's Courage Shopping List:

....

....

....

....

....

....

....

....

....

....

....

....

....

....

....

....

....

....

Hero's short and long-term visions:

....
....
....
....
....
....
....
....
....
....
....
....
....
....
....
....
....

THANK YOU

Driver: "It doesn't get better than this! From the moment we are born, we are blessed with everything helping us survive.

We've come a long way, haven't we? I hope you enjoyed the power ride in the Mustang GT through time and its powerful insights into 'The survival system' and its survival forces. Too realistic to be fiction? Too fictitious to be real? What do you think?

Power to you, power to the little kid and the teenager in you... in the 21st Century.

Here's to you reinventing yourself, embracing your potential and forging an independent path with your Higher wisdom, your updated, high-octane self-image and the courage to cross off each item on your courage shopping list. ☺

Will you have the courage to be 'The Hero' in your story? Will you defy the stigma of the 'Midlife Crisis' label and upgrade your life to one of emotional independence, personal power and free will and live the second half of your life on your terms, with or without approval?

Give yourself permission to be great!"

COURSE HANDOUTS:

HANDOUT 1: SURVIVAL AND YOUR SUBCONSCIOUS MIND

Although there are many books available on how to work with your subconscious mind, let's add more understanding of its importance from a *survival, reactive perspective* and how it relates to our lives today.

Did you know?

- The subconscious mind is pro-life and has been helping us survive since the beginning of time.

- The subconscious mind was our survival memory before our intellectual brain evolved.

- **The subconscious mind is still our survival memory in the first seven years of every child's life, before our intellectual brain takes over!**

- The subconscious mind does not recognise or respond to the intellect... no matter our age!

- The subconscious mind does not conform to man's rules or man's time.

- Your subconscious mind is always on alert, ready to work for you.

Your subconscious mind has been compared to a six-year-old child:

- It cannot reason, question, discriminate or make distinctions.

- It lives in its literal world, believing everything you say, trusting you and your words, especially those spoken with *emotional intensity* – be careful what you say and what you wish for.

- It loves repetition and images.

When you think of your subconscious mind, think of a 'literal, serious and personal' world of a six-year-old child living in its own time zone.

The distinction between a subconscious reaction and a memory:

Subconscious reactions are fast, automatic, subliminal reactions directing you to believe, feel or act in a particular way to your present situation.

Memories are reminders of something from your past, not directing you to do anything. They are usually attached to your senses e.g., the smell of a roast dinner cooking taking you back to family gatherings, a song reminding you of someone special or reminiscing about a joyful or sad event etc.

HANDOUT 2: HOW TO WORK WITH YOUR SUBCONSCIOUS MIND TODAY

What does your subconscious mind love to work with?

- Repetition

- Images

- Passion and emotional intensity.

How are you contributing to your current situation?

When your subconscious hears you say frequently with passion and emotional intensity, things like:

- *"I'm always experiencing delays!"* or

- *"I can never have what I want!"* or

- *"I'm always in debt!"*

Guess what! You will get more of the same. Your subconscious believes that is what you want. It's literal! It takes you at your word!

How to work with and benefit from your subconscious:

- Become aware of your internal dialogue.

- Use positive, simple words that cannot be misinterpreted – remember, your subconscious can be likened to a six-year-old child.

- Use short direct sentences/statements.

- *Speak and feel with emotional intensity.*

- Visualise images of yourself with the item you are seeking.

- Concentrate on one item at a time.

- Repeat your statement over and over every day – especially upon waking and before you go to sleep.

- Continue repeating your statement until you get what you want.

Be sincere. You can't trick kids on an emotional level – that's their language and the language of your subconscious mind.

Don't decide how you think 'it' should happen – your subconscious doesn't work with your intellect, rules, beliefs or traditional thinking. Watch out for the unexpected.

Don't decide how long 'it' should take – your subconscious has no clocks or watches in its world.

Decide what it is you are seeking or wanting to change. Construct your short, passionate, simple sentence using the above format.

Your request is now out of your hands and your learnt controlling behaviour. Stay alert for clues. Be patient and keep the faith. Know your subconscious is devoted to you and is doing everything in its power to deliver your wish. Let your subconscious do its job. Persistence and dedication wins!

HANDOUT 3: SELF-TALK AND AFFIRMATIONS

Motivating and coaching yourself is the voice of your personal power.

Positive self-talk and affirmations is a great fear diffuser and are powerful, portable allies, available 24/7, helping overcome self-doubt, childhood insecurities and emotional obstacles, whenever you need encouragement and motivation.

Become aware of your internal dialogue. Note the words and phrases you use frequently when speaking to yourself. Are they loving words and phrases, boosting your confidence and encouraging you?

Now let's add some powerful, personally meaningful affirmations to help you build your 'dream-team' confidence with your inner child:

- "I love taking charge of our life."

- *"My fears are mostly perceived fears. They can't hurt us."*

- "The next step will be so empowering for us."

- *"I love conquering our fears."*

- "Our fears and self-doubts are mainly from childhood."

- *"We're ready to take on more responsibility."*

- *"There's no such thing as certainty. Trying is our new success."*

- "I understand what is holding us back. We give it no power."

- *"We adapt to change easily."*

- "We are ready to go beyond childhood limits."

- *"We are so much more than we ever dared to believe."*

- "We can handle anything that comes our way."

- *"We feel safe and secure together."*

- "We are ready to face our future with new confidence."

- *"I love to feel my power."*

- "It's great to own my power."

- *"We give ourselves permission to be great!"*

Any others?

. . . .

. . . .

. . . .

Continue encouraging yourself and your inner child. Talk softly, gently and lovingly to the little kid in you: *"Come on kiddo, we can do this! We're bigger than this situation."*

You are becoming your own life coach and creating your future today.

Don't forget to praise and congratulate yourself regularly on your progress.

HANDOUT 4: A TRIBUTE TO YOUR INNER CHILD

I love my inner child's primal simplicity –
Her beliefs in the first seven years created our history.
My inner child believes she is all she can be...
She is the younger version of me.

I see everything through my inner child's eyes...
Her beliefs become my beliefs until I am wise.
She is dependent and powerless in every way –
I show her there's more when I shoo fear away.

With her by my side I make perfect sense...
She is the substance, the heart and the core of my essence.
Our 'dream-team' consciousness transforms my identity.
I am complete and transcending my inner child's destiny.

Louise L. Kallaway.

HANDOUT EXTRA: PERSONAL REASONS FOR FEELING 'STUCK' & POWERLESS

What's been happening in your life lately?

- Have you had a huge disappointment; loss of a job, a dream, a love affair that hasn't worked out for you? How have any of these or similar scenarios been impacting you?

- Are you depressed? Depression is anger turned inwards. There is no loudness or aggression, but rather a quiet, all-embracing feeling of despondency. Are you angry with yourself? Do you know why?

- Have you not been feeling well lately – physically, emotionally, mentally? What impact has this been having on you?

- Do you feel there is something missing from your life? Anything nagging at you?

- Have you been feeling overwhelmed, even defeated? Defeat can manifest as a sense of hopelessness, most often resulting in inactivity.

- Any other personal reasons?

Acknowledging what is impacting you or holding you back will set you free. It usually has something to do with expanding your emotional life... remember, your emotional life is your courage.

HERO WORSHIP

Driver: "Have you wondered how Hero is today? We remember his pain, don't we? We witnessed the many enlightened moments that unlocked Hero's frustration which was his goal for attending *'The Mastering Course'*. But also, to his surprise, he grew to admire anyone called out as having a Midlife Crisis. To Hero, that would be his ultimate success!

Well, I received an email from Hero yesterday. He said on his return home, he faithfully did his homework and for the first time in years, he felt invigorated and excited about his life and his prospects.

He said, the question on the Handouts Extra re overwhelm and feeling defeated really got him thinking. He went on to say he now thinks the powerlessness he thought he was feeling when he enrolled in *'The Mastering Course'* was more like a sense of hopelessness, even despair, resulting in inactivity and just getting by in the last few years.

It's now my pleasure to tell everyone, Hero has been called out as having his Midlife Crisis! He said he was absolutely delighted ☺ He now considers himself to be an independent, empowered adult who is no longer willing to go along with the crowd on matters that are important in his life. He said he is starting his own business, remaining in the profession he loves so much, but moving in a new and exciting direction. He said he's sooo ready for a change and a challenge! Apparently, he wrote 'Career move?' on his Courage Shopping List and this was the result.

Hero said he now recognises that the people who called him out as having a Midlife Crisis are 'stuck' in their Childhood Model just like he was; he feels their frustration too. Hero has tried talking to them and he even recommended *'The Mastering Course'* but… their need to belong, fear of rejection and what others might say, has them living frustratingly under their potential, **fearful of their own liberation.**

Hero also wants us to know there's been some interesting changes and huge positive inroads in his relationship with his parents, especially his father. He said when he told his family at lunch that he was going to start his own business, he thought he'd be howled down, but instead, his father took him to one side saying, *"We are very proud of you"*, congratulating him on his self-belief and courage. He then confided that he joined the family business as a young man because he liked the security and the status and he wasn't prepared to stand up against the family tradition of the eldest son taking over the business.

His father admitted that his daughter, Hero's sister, is doing a fabulous job of following in the family footsteps, winning more than 95% of her court cases, which is a remarkable achievement. His father further admitted, it has taken him 15 years to shake off old generational thinking that it must be the eldest son who takes over the family business! More proof that 'old generational beliefs die hard'.

His father now wants to be part of our Hero's endeavours and is offering his financial and emotional support and legal advice on how best to set up his company.

Hero asked if we would like to hear more of his successes and any conflicts he has overcome. I emailed him immediately on behalf of the Team, congratulating him on his Midlife Crisis ☺ and the new and 'equal' relationship he is now enjoying, especially with his father. I wrote, 'Yes please! We'd love to hear from you. You are such an inspiration to us.'

Cheers to happy endings…

Bubbles anyone?"

ABOUT THE AUTHOR

Hello. Thank you for taking your time to read 'About the author'. Living my whole life on Planet Earth and not understanding how it works would have been unthinkable for me. I must have accepted 'The Mission' before I arrived on earth because I was born into the perfect set of circumstances and the family to do 'My purpose' justice...

I doubt anything is random in life. That is not to say we don't have free will, but when we are truly committed to a cause, a purpose, an outcome and when it becomes an all-consuming passion... our destiny will not be denied.

My fascination into 'The survival system' we were born into came to light in my difficult teenage years. As a child then teenager, I saw firsthand generational cycles repeating themselves through my mother and her little brother's childhood experiences as Wards of the State of New South Wales, Australia, during the Great Depression. Those little kids were four and three years old respectively, when they were abruptly taken from the family home and handed, like a baton, to someone they had never met, in a state system that was, by today's standards, emotionally harsh... some say cruel and insensitive.

Imagine their terror! Abandonment is a primal fear. No assurances would have been given to a child or children taken from their family in that era; that they will be safe and supported by their new carers! How terrifying! You want to give them assurances and a big hug, don't you?

At 16, I questioned why my mother repeated her fearful, defensive, angry and loveless childhood that hurt her so much, to her innocent kids. My brother, sister and I all lived our mother's childhood traumas of feeling unsafe, unloved and unworthy, *as if we were the children made Wards of the State!*

***

I am not a psychologist; I am a researcher. My analytical and logical conclusions into why generational cycles repeat themselves have been deduced from 30 years of research and study into 'The survival system' we inherited. I have found no evidence to suggest psychology played a role in our survival. Life-sculpting survival programs are simple, non-intellectual, repetitive and reactive.

It becomes a problem for us today in our maturing years as we live two, three, even four years longer than our primitive cousins, with an evolving intellectual brain. Today we are being stunted and dumbed down by a non-intellectual survival system, borne into our DNA, that was designed for what is now only the first half of our lives.

'The survival system' gave its power to 'The group' and a conforming mentality. With this understanding, it becomes clear, how and why the odds are stacked against 'The maturing individual' ever achieving his independence and potential in the 21st Century! Conforming with the rules of 'The group', no matter who they are, is the number one issue in all stages of our lives… until we have the courage to liberate our own freedom.

To ignore evolving discoveries and pretend this research doesn't exist, is what the status quo does. That's its job! To keep us safe, living within 'The Pack' and its united we stand mentality, maintaining order and resisting change of any kind… and so, perpetuating mediocrity. We remain part of the status quo when we choose to be silent above making a difference in our community or by making better, more empowering choices for ourselves and our loved ones.

Without people like you who are willing to investigate new possibilities, the world will remain stagnant in the hands of the status quo. If *T!me…* has helped make sense of your life, imagine how it could help people with anger issues, depression and/or suicidal thoughts, feelings of 'stuckness' and powerlessness etc. to make sense of their lives too.

***

I may be contacted at www.linkedin.com/in/louise-l-kallaway or through my website: www.louiselkallaway.com

Other 'Life Education' books and journals in this series:

- Empowered – Secrets of your inner child

- Defiance – Secrets of your midlife crisis

- Evolving – Secrets of a child and life processes

- You and your inner child today… Journal

- Conscious – How life works… Journal

- Survival – How fear works… Journal

- Once Upon a T!me… How life's story becomes your story.